MW01120337

Action Leads to Success
The Book on Leadership

Dear Gajan

You are amazing

Kula

Kula Sellathurai & Raymond Aaron

Copyright © 2017 Kula Sellathurai and Raymond Aaron

ISBN: 978-1544049724

All rights reserved. No portion of this book may be reproduced mechanically, electronically, or by any other means, including photocopying, without permission of the publisher or author except in the case of brief quotations embodied in critical articles and reviews. It is illegal to copy this book, post it to a website, or distribute it by any other means without permission from the publisher or author.

Limits of Liability and Disclaimer of Warranty
The author and publisher shall not be liable for your misuse of the enclosed material. This book is strictly for informational and educational purposes only.

Warning – Disclaimer
The purpose of this book is to educate and entertain. The author and/or publisher do not guarantee that anyone following these techniques, suggestions, tips, ideas, or strategies will become successful. The author and/or publisher shall have neither liability nor responsibility to anyone with respect to any loss or damage caused, or alleged to be caused, directly or indirectly by the information contained in this book.

Publisher
10-10-10 Publishing
Markham, ON
Canada

Contents

Dedication   v

Foreword   vii

Introduction   ix

Note From Co-Author   xi

Testimonials   xiii

Chapter 1: Have a Purpose and Vision   1

Chapter 2: Think Big   11

Chapter 3: Set High Standards, Be Uncomfortable   23

Chapter 4: Be Practical, Logical, and Tough   35

Chapter 5: Be Enthusiastic and Expressive   47

Chapter 6: Focus on the Next Move   53

Chapter 7: Be Tolerant and Empathetic   63

Chapter 8: Have High Energy   75

Chapter 9: Be Charismatic and Influential   81

Chapter 10: Act Fast, Act Bold   93

Chapter 11: Keep Everyone Motivated   105

Chapter 12: Have a Sense of Humor   113

Dedication

I dedicate this book to the following people …

First and foremost, I would like to recognize my late parents. They sacrificed most of their adult life to educate and feed me and my six siblings, putting in far more effort and enduring much more sacrifice than we will have to do for our own children. And even though they are not with us today, I must express my sincere gratitude to them for bringing me up to be who I am today.

My older brother Bala, who put me on a plane to Canada; who put me on the path to my success.

Mr. Gord Matineau—a news anchor at City TV. I learned to speak the English language fluently and, later, to speak on stages by watching him present the evening news. He was much more than just a news reader. He was a very interesting and stylish news presenter.

My best friend ever, Mr. Ganesan Sugumar, a successful serial entrepreneur who coached and supported me for more than two decades.

Last but not least, my beautiful wife Sanjula and daughter Akshaya. They've been behind me through every step and sacrifice, losing lots of family time and not having me there with them whenever they most needed me. This book would not be a reality without them.

Foreword

Kula Sellathurai and Raymond Aaron are both leaders, successful businessmen and serial entrepreneurs. This book, *Action Leads to Success,* is their way of giving back some of the wonderful things that have happened in their life. They will cover difficult topics such as setting high standards and learning to be comfortable with change by learning how to be uncomfortable in the moment so that you can reach a more comfortable place in the future. It sounds simple but is so, so hard to do.

The authors want you to think big, act bold and act fast. Not blindly, though. They want you to know and understand your purpose, to have a vision that carries you forward with the power of someone living and acting on purpose. This will require many things of you: Kula and Raymond show you how and why you need to be practical, logical and tough, yet they are champions of the ideas of being enthusiastic, expressive, charismatic and empathetic.

Kula and Raymond don't forget the energy that living on purpose demands. Nor do they shy away from tough topics like focus and being influential. This is a book that is as clear as an empty highway, but it also shows you how to maneuver the eventual potholes, turnpikes and roadblocks. I recommend *Action Leads to Success* so that you can make a difference in your world.

This book will teach you the key to getting the most from all the leadership learning activities to coordinate them. Know what knowledge, skills and experiences you need, and plan how to acquire them in an integrated fashion.

Adam Markel
CEO, New Peaks
Author of *Pivot*

Introduction

Kula Sellathurai has been an entrepreneur for more than two decades and is now a successful business coach. The past President of the Canadian Tamils' Chamber of Commerce, Chairman and Past President of the Canada-Sri Lanka Business Council and a Medal Recipient to Her Majesty Queen Elizabeth II Diamond Jubilee, this talented man is now the author of this powerful new treatise, *Action Leads to Success: The Book on Leadership.*

Have a Purpose and Vision

Just how does action lead to success? A great leader will always have a purpose and vision for themselves and will be ready to act when the situation demands that they do so. Such leaders are few and far between. Why is that? The average person does not go through life taking action on purpose. No, the average person reacts to what the day brings, while the leader responds to what they see or experience, making moment-to-moment choices based on their intended purpose and vision.

Think Big

To think like a leader, you must instill in yourself the belief that you are of great help to people in all aspects of their lives. The choices a great leader makes usually involve being actively aware of what's going on around them, identifying problems or opportunities to perpetuate their vision of themselves. As a leader, your potential will be recognized as you see the problems that are too great to overcome or too small to ponder.

Set High Standards, Be Uncomfortable

The leader sets the bar high. This is done because you understand that great results and rewards lie just beyond the edge of what you may find comfortable. Thus, you are willing to purposefully cross the line and embrace the unknown.

Be Practical, Logical and Tough

One must know that as a leader you are logical to the nth degree, each choice being made on purpose, aligned with your vision. This helps to create a certain mental toughness, also necessary for great leadership.

Focus on the Next Move

The leader is someone who, once the decision to act is made, is already focused on their next move. Massive action does not happen by accident. It requires a strong mental presence. It also requires a significant amount of energy. How else are you to constantly make the right decision from moment to moment? Believe it or not you must also learn to be tolerant of others who do not have the skill set you have. You could go on to say that a certain level of empathy for other people is necessary, just as charisma and an ability to influence others is important to have.

Act Fast; Act Bold

One last thing: The leader is a master of action and knows the importance of acting fast and acting bold, of knocking out the competition with their brazenly beautiful symphony of purposeful action.

So, read on and learn from one of the best …

Note From Co-Author

Having met many inspirational authors in my time, I can safely say that I know a good writer when I meet one. Kula Sellathurai is such an author. His words will drive meaning into your heart, and they will inspire the change that you dream of achieving in your life.

Sellathurai speaks with your voice; you, who has the drive and desire to build a great life, both in your personal relationships and in your professional career. His words will resonate with you, who have felt like you have a greater purpose in life than simply being another cog in the wheel. This book is the culmination of his extensive and varied experience, and it has been my great pleasure to see it come to publication.

If you seek greater satisfaction with your everyday life, if you feel disenfranchised with your current direction, or simply wish to create a lasting difference in this world, I cannot recommend this book enough. Sellathurai's emotive and informative writing is captivating, and will challenge you to find a higher purpose in your daily life. I am already looking forward to see what Sellathurai creates in the future.

Raymond Aaron
New York Times Bestselling Author

Testimonials

"Must read for those who aspire and strive to achieve! Kula well captures the essence of leadership. He ably captures the element of leadership, and defines not just the WHAT, but also the HOW of leading. Kula brings to life the realities of leading, while being led....a guide to all who are running up the rungs of leadership."
M. Suranjan
President, P&G Asia Pacific

"Mr. Sellathurai draws on his wealth of personal experience as a successful businessman, community leader and philanthropist to draw a concrete and complete road map to success for motivated individuals. In *Action Leads to Success,* he goes to great lengths to stress that leadership is not an innate skill, but one that is the product of diligence, fortitude and humility. In so doing, he demonstrates that the ability to lead is within all of us, however only if we are prepared to do the hard work that is required."
Paul Kelly
Criminal Lawyer, Toronto

"*Action Leads to Success* is an insightful analysis of the concept of leadership. Kula Sellathurai provides a practical road guide illuminating the issues and potential problems faced by individuals who aspire to lead. His easy to understand solutions will benefit anyone who seeks the success that comes from the long-term recognition and respect as a leader."
Tony Loparco
Director, SIU

Chapter 1

Have a Purpose and Vision

Some time ago, I was part of a transformational training program and was attending a week long marketing seminar. There were many speakers, presenters and coaches teaching us all throughout the week long course. Near the close of the final day, all of us were feeling the 100 degrees sizzling hot energy in the room; our lead trainer Adam started our final session by asking all of us to share our experiences from the week and to ask any questions we still had.

The microphone was being passed from one attendee to the other until it was finally given to a man named Joe. He picked up the microphone and without preamble said, "I ignored my sister's calls for the past three weeks because of my busy lifestyle, and I just got the news this morning that she passed away. I hate myself."

The entire class went dead silent. The atmosphere changed from that of high sizzling energy to a near frozen state. No one knew what to say or do, but in that moment I saw the leader in Adam come out. He directed us to sit down while he walked over to Joe. He looked Joe square in the eyes and told him that what happened is not his fault and then made him understand the reality of the situation. In that moment Adam made an impact in Joe's life, moving him from a path that could have ended with Joe hurting himself or living with guilt for the rest of his life, and instead making him see the situation from a different viewpoint.

That moment gave me the title for this book; I saw Adam and marked then that there was a spontaneous leader. A few moments later he turned back to the group and, having helped Joe come to terms with his sister's death, Adam brought us back to the sizzling energy that he had inspired in us before. His leadership helped us all that week and extended far beyond into our lives.

A leader will always have a purpose and vision for himself or herself and will be ready to act when the situation demands someone to take control. You can become prepared to step into this role and handle any such situation that may arise through developing your visionary thinking.

With this mental attitude, you can become a leader who can make spur-of-the-moment decisions that others cannot. Such leaders seldom experience anxiety in the moment and are confident that their actions and decisions are exactly what need to be done.

A leader will always give himself or herself constructive criticism in order to grow the ability to lead, by acknowledging both their strengths and weaknesses. Your purpose and vision will have a clear direction of the path that you will follow, along which you can bring those who are ready to follow.

Leaders are rarely born; they are made. Persistence and circumstance play a bigger role in developing a great leader than initial circumstances ever will, so it is this discipline that you must work on, building within your personality. Only through determined development will you ensure that you are able to rise up in moments of crisis when a leader is needed.

You must also always be able to adapt to different leadership styles, and to know what skills and expertise are particularly useful in each individual situation.

Therefore, you must anticipate what skills you will need, and then learn to acquire them along the way. Good thoughts and actions can never produce bad results; the true result of leadership is not how far you can advance but how far you can advance others alongside you by serving and adding value to their lives. A good leader will see through a lens that others cannot see, and make them follow in the right direction.

Fifteen years ago, I was the president of a Community Chamber of Commerce that was celebrating its 10th year anniversary. I was given the task of organizing the celebrations and wanted to make it an event to remember. I wanted this celebration to bring a good name to our community and enhance our reputation across the country. The Chamber had less than two hundred members and was dependent on its membership revenues in order to keep operating, so as a result of this, we had less than five thousand dollars in our bank account and the budget that I had drawn up called for seventy-five thousand. When I announced this to the community many senior members were very against my proposal, claiming that there was no way that we could raise that type of money. But there were a few influential members who believed in me when the plan was laid out and encouraged me to go ahead with my ambitions.

I decided to reach out to the big banks for sponsorship, managing to secure a lunch meeting with the Vice President of one of the largest banks in the country. We met at one of the finest restaurants in the area for lunch, and once we were seated and welcomed, the waiter turned to me and welcomed me in my mother language, Tamil. I was surprised at first, but replied back in Tamil and chatted briefly before we proceeded with our orders. After the waiter had left the table, the banker turned to me in surprise and I told her that such a thing was an example of the power of a community. I told her how the community environment encouraged restaurants to teach their staff to greet us in our own language, elaborating how a partnership with the bank could only improve this already positive process.

Throughout the entire lunch I had butterflies running through my stomach, but by the time we had finished our meal, I had convinced the banker to sponsor our event with a significant sum of money. After that, it was much easier to convince other sponsors to join alongside the bank, and in the end we were able to host a large and very successful anniversary event. As I left the restaurant that fateful first day, I praised the leader within me for helping turn a potentially embarrassing situation into an extremely positive outcome.

At the end of the day, what we all wish to feel is useful and respected.

We look to the great leaders of the past such as Gandhi, Martin Luther King Jr., Rosa Parks and so many more and we see how they led those around them forward in pursuit of the collective goal. We see how they were revered and praised by the common man who saw in them the greatness of what a united front could achieve. And so we push forward to create for ourselves this same life of respect and success. I tell you now that all these things can be yours if you simply believe in yourself. You must know that your purpose is true, your faith is well founded and your goal is achievable. When you embrace your full potential, you will understand that you can achieve that which you fully set your mind to and so much more. You will go beyond your comfort zone, forging ahead to create a new area in which you might initially be uncomfortable, but in time that you will feel secure in. This broadening of your abilities will only happen over time, though, and so you must have faith that it will develop if you trust in yourself and continue to refine your skills.

There will be times when you feel like you are drained, exhausted and cannot continue pushing forward. It may seem at times like you are faltering and will see that others around appear to have overtaken you and pushed further ahead. When this happens, you must stand resolute and continue on with your goal no matter how the situation looks. In times like this, remember the tale of *The Tortoise and The Hare* in Aesop's Fables.

As the story goes, the Hare was boastful and arrogant, constantly praising himself publicly for all that he could do. Tired of the Hare's unending self-praise, the Tortoise decides that he will challenge the Hare to a race. As expected, the Hare soon leaves the Tortoise behind and is so confident in his inevitable victory that he decides to take a nap part way through the race. Resolute, the Tortoise pushes on, worrying not about the Hare but only on his own performance. With this determination, the Tortoise passes the sleeping Hare and continues on to the finish line, much to the pleasant surprise of those looking on. The Hare awakens to these cheers and, realizing his mistake, rushes to the finish line but it is far too late. The resolute and determined Tortoise had pushed on and completed what he set out to do.

Stories like this may have come from long ago fables but they are still so relevant in our modern world today. Look and you will find pages in the history books of long ago heroes and leaders who pushed on no matter how the odds stacked against them. Have faith in yourself, take pride in your accomplishments and you will eventually achieve your goals. Stay hungry, determined and humble and know that what you are going for is a just and honorable goal. When others see your immense drive to accomplish what you set your mind on, they will be unable to turn away, and will be swept up in the wake you leave behind you. In these moments, you will become the leader that you know in your heart you can truly be.

There are also personal goals that you, as a prospective leader, can work on to prepare you for situations that often arise for leaders of various kinds. These are more of a common catch-list of goals for leaders, but they should not be ignored …

Personal Goals for Spontaneous Leaders

1. Strategic vs. Tactical Thinking. Improve your ability to see the big picture and take a longer range, broader business perspective. Learn to step back from the day-to-day tactical details of your business and focus on the "why", not just the "what" and "how." I'm not saying that you should walk away from tactical details. What I am saying is that there is merit in the daily exercise of working to understand why problems arise and if they are just part of the business model or if there are actual problems that present as opportunities for a spontaneous leader.

2. Communication/Listening. Learn to pay attention to what is being said and then demonstrate to others that that you value what they have to say. Use active listening (fully concentrating on what is being said rather than just passively 'hearing' the message of the speaker. Active listening involves listening with all senses. As well as giving full attention to the speaker, it is important that the 'active listener' is also 'seen' to be listening—otherwise the speaker may conclude that what they are talking about is uninteresting to the listener. Interest can be conveyed to the speaker by using both verbal and non-verbal messages such as maintaining eye contact, nodding your head and smiling, agreeing by saying 'Yes' or simply 'Mmm hmm' to encourage them to continue. By providing this 'feedback' the person speaking will usually feel more at ease and therefore communicate more easily, openly and honestly.), use open-ended questions (questions that cannot be answered with a yes or no) and eliminate distractions that get in the way of your ability to listen.

3. Coaching. Shift your leadership style away from always directing and telling and learn to guide and develop those who report directly to you. Work with each of these people, helping them to create their own individual development plans.

4. Financial Acumen. Learn how to understand, interpret, and use "the numbers" to improve your business. There are just a handful of formulas to learn in order to understand financial reports generated by accountants or that already exist as part of your business plan. Leaders are expected to know business numbers by heart; employees and managers are truly supported by a leader who can demonstrate he or she has the ship under control and heading in the right direction.

5. Know Your Business. Learn about other aspects of the business other than normally fall under my purvue. The business plan is a good place to begin; the marketing plan should be next. A spontaneous leader knows every cog and wheel in the business or knows where to put his or her finger on that knowledge quickly and effortlessly.

6. Industry Knowledge. Improve your understanding of your industry and your competitors. Get closer to your customers and find out what they need and value.

7. Leadership Presence. Improve your ability to "command a room" and communicate in an authentic way that inspires others. Follow the following simple steps …

a) Show up early or precisely on time—never late. Walking in late means you need an apology and an excuse before you say anything else. It's not a strong starting position, and it can be difficult to overcome no matter how great your reasons might be.

b) Enter the room with intention. As you arrive at the door, pause for a moment with your head up to survey the scene. Move purposefully toward the seat you want, which will vary depending on the purpose of the gathering and the room arrangement.

c) Ground yourself by putting both feet on the floor and sitting squarely in your seat. Plan to slouch later.

d) Use your polished "go to" introduction to say who you are without fluff or mumbles.

e) Each time you speak, project your voice to the farthest person in the room. No, you're not shouting. It just feels like that.

f) Complete all requested prework ahead of time. If you do, you'll be able to answer a definitive "yes" when the presenter asks, "Did everyone get the materials and read them?" Completing preparatory work will differentiate you from most other people in the room and sets the bar higher for the group in future meetings.

g) Bring both your knowledge and curiosity. Use a tactic from the professional coach's playbook and ask open-ended questions to encourage discussion.

h) Have an opinion. Having an opinion demonstrates that you've been paying attention and that you care.

i) Concisely state your perspective. If you typically have an opinion but struggle to articulate it in a compelling way, write it down beforehand. Be prepared to also clearly say why. Know upfront what you feel passionate about and what you can live with if it doesn't go your way.

8. Change. Be a champion of change. Be a catalyst. Learn to implement and sustain change in your organization.

9. Remote Management. Improve your ability to manage your remote, reporting staff members. Make better use of technology to plan, communicate and collaborate virtually.

10. Collaboration. Improve relationships with your peers. Be a better partner, understand their goals and needs, and learn to work together to help achieve each other's goals.

Chapter 2
Think Big

In this chapter I will outline the ways in which you must think in order to make yourself into a good leader. This begins with training your own beliefs and practices to create and cultivate a mentality of leadership. Obtaining this leading mentality is a crucial early step in becoming a successful leader, as it paves the way for a lifetime of leadership. Once this mentality is ingrained within you, you will then learn the concept of "thinking big", which will be a valuable asset in your leadership campaign.

In order to become a true leader you must first learn to think like one. A leader is confident, and thinks of himself in terms of his own worth to others. This means you must believe that others need your prowess in order to succeed. Thus, you must think of yourself as an asset with great amounts of untapped talent, just waiting to be given the opportunity you deserve, and you will find that opportunity presents itself. Do not lose hope if you fail to find opportunities right away rather, use the time to strengthen your resolve and persevere in your journey to success.

To think like a leader you must instill in yourself the belief that you are of great help to people in all aspects of their lives. Do not discount any problem as too insignificant to ponder, or too great to tackle. As a leader, you should simply be there for others, to help them no matter what. If you believe in yourself and your own ability to solve problems on a broad scale, other people will put faith in your ability to help them with their own specific problems and duties. Then, when people put their faith in you, you will be granted the opportunities you deserve and you will be able to show your true potential.

In addition to believing in your own professional ability, you must also believe that helping people adds value to their lives and that both you and the people you help can achieve a sense of fulfillment and satisfaction from the work you do. This will strengthen your sense of self-worth, and will make you more appealing as a leader in the eyes of others. If you come off as appealing, charismatic, and hard-working, you will be renowned among your peers as a strong leader.

As a leader you should not be doing all of this only for the promise of a monetary reward. Try to avoid placing a dollar value on the services you provide as this will stunt your growth as a leader. Instead, you must believe that the financial reward is the impact you have on the lives of others due to your influence. Placing a heightened value on experience and influence will make you a better leader, and financial rewards will come with hard work and perseverance once your leadership abilities are known.

Once you have crafted this mentality of leadership, other people will view you as a leader and an asset. If you instill these beliefs in yourself, others will come to you to learn from you and to follow in your footsteps.

You must make yourself into a strong role model for others and compel them to want to be like you. Overall, you must believe that you deserve responsibility, respect, and adoration; this is the true essence of a mentality of leadership.

In order to become a successful leader, a leader that is desirable to the people around you, you will need to put your leadership mentality into practice. You will need to focus on finding problems that others are having, and devising pragmatic solutions to them. This means that you will need to seek out people that are having problems, and be the leader they need in order to aid them. You must come up with ingenious yet simple solutions to these daily pains of others to make yourself a successful leader. If you can provide help for people in this way, you will be known as a leader to those around you, and people will seek you out whenever they have a problem that needs solving. The smaller responsibilities you take on in order to help out your peers, the more people will view you as a good leader and, as a result, you will find yourself presented with bigger opportunities and responsibilities.

If you have succeeded in forming yourself into an individual with good problem-solving abilities and the mentality of a leader, you must now focus on becoming a "big thinker". This means that, on top of your belief in yourself as a leader, you must convince others that your ideas will help them attain their goals. Thinking big is a key stage in progressing as a leader, and you will find yourself stagnated if you do not master this skill.

To become a big thinker, you must be creative and imaginative, while also being practical and keeping the needs of others in mind. Some big ideas are controversial, and this is fine; people will come around once they realize you possess the qualities of a leader and they know you can and will follow through with your ideas. If you believe that you are an asset to others, as you should, then you must also convince others that you are an asset to them. Being confident, persuasive, and convincing is another essential skill you will need to learn in order to succeed as a leader, as it will aid you in your quest to have your ideas heard by the masses.

You need to sell yourself as a leader, as someone that can provide a necessary service to others, and someone that will change their lives for the better while keeping their best interests at heart. This multiplicity of roles that you must upkeep in your journey to become a better leader will be tough, but you must remember that no task is too much for you to handle. If you have difficulties, face them head-on with no fear and you will find that tackling problems such as these will improve your life, both as a leader and as an individual. Keeping a healthy balance between tending to your own responsibilities and tending to the interests of others is a necessary skill that you must acquire in order to be a successful leader.

Another essential skill you must learn in your journey to successful leadership is that of forming bonds with your peers and creating allies that form mutually beneficial relationships. Keeping people on your side in this way will automatically make it easier to help you succeed as a leader. Furthermore, keeping people on your side will give you the recognition of your leadership, which will provide you with personal satisfaction and let you know that you are on the right track.

To be clear, you should not attempt to become a leader only to achieve adoration among your peers rather, you must become a leader in the hopes of improving your own life and the lives of everyone around you. Allies will aid you in your journey to becoming a successful leader, but only if they know that your intentions are true and pure. Having allies that turn to you for help will build your reputation as a leader, and you will become more well-known and desired among others as a result.

As a leader, you must not be afraid to take chances in your life. A skill you must learn in this journey to becoming a successful leader is having the willpower to take chances despite any apprehension you may feel.

You must accept the fact that your ideas are good ones, and if you believe in yourself, you will know that taking chances will produce positive results. If you take a chance and it backfires, do not be discouraged rather, accept your mistake and learn from it. Accepting your mistakes is another key characteristic of a good leader, and other people will be impressed by you if you master this skill and use your mistakes to improve your performance in the future.

To be a successful leader and a big thinker you need to take big chances, even if they may seem risky. Every great leader in history has taken huge chances that posed huge risks to make themselves what they were, and to foster their legacies. As a leader, you must use your ability to think big and come up with ingenious ideas that will resonate for generations.

You must remember that you will never get anywhere by being overly cautious. It is good to think about the consequences of your actions, but do not let this consideration turn you into a leader without confidence. Taking big chances is a good thing and it will improve your leadership qualities, especially when taking that big chance pays off and you are given a promising opportunity. Keep in mind that none of this is possible without learning to become a big thinker—big ideas will produce incredible results, and if you are successful in this vein, the people around you will see you as a strong leader.

Attaining a high level of passion for what you do is essential in your journey to become a good leader. Your work must reflect something about yourself so that it becomes a vessel through which you can channel your passion. Remember that opportunities will only present themselves to you if people see you as a strong leader. Once you are passionate about whatever project you are faced with when you are presented with these opportunities, and you clearly understand why you are devoting your time to the project, your life will become noticeably easier.

In essence, passion is one of the most important things that a successful leader can possess. This is because it is far easier to do a good job on a project you are passionate about, than to try and do a good job on a project that you think is irrelevant. Channeling your passion into your work is a necessary skill that all leaders must possess, because passion breeds success. Once other people realize the true passion you have for your work, they will follow you in whatever endeavors you choose, and they will continue to present you with opportunities because they will believe in you.

Being a leader is obviously not an easy task, and you will inevitably find yourself encountering some problems or roadblocks on your journey. Thus, it is important for you to accept the reality that you will face certain problems in order to adequately prepare yourself for tackling them. These roadblocks can appear in many forms, small or large, and you must be equipped to handle them and get over them in order to become a successful leader.

Roadblocks will present themselves in many areas throughout your life, and as a leader, you must learn to deal with these roadblocks in a professional manner. The best thing to do when you initially encounter a roadblock in any instance is first to accept the situation. Do not become disgruntled; you must understand that as a leader, you can solve any problems with which you are presented, and that includes unforeseen problems of your own.

This is not to say that as a leader you must become isolated. Do not be afraid to seek help and advice from others if you are in need. When faced with a roadblock you may seek advice from others if you so desire, and then you must put together a plan with a clear goal in mind to tackle your problem. Once you know what your plan is, you must follow it until you are exactly where you want to be. If it is necessary, revise your plan as many times as needed, but do not stop until you have reached your goal. Changing your tactics in order to solve a problem is fine and often necessary – knowing when to change your approach is the quality of a true leader. However, it is important to note that you must not change your goal in this process. If you change your goal it makes a statement that you are indecisive or not willing to put in your full effort to tackle a problem. This will cause people to lose their trust and faith in you, as it shows that you do not possess the necessary resolve that a leader should have when faced with a complex task. If you understand your goal when you are first presented with a problem, and you strive to reach that goal no matter what, people will know that you are reliable, and they will trust you and follow you.

As a leader, one of your most advantageous qualities will be a penchant for self-evaluation. It is a valuable skill to teach yourself, and you should always re-evaluate your own ideas with constructive criticism. This will not only improve your problem-solving abilities in the long-run, and but also will open you up to accepting constructive criticism from others.

Leadership means never believing that your ideas are perfect, and always trying to better yourself in the interest of providing a better service to others. Even if you have a good idea, you should still brainstorm ways that your idea can be improved because no idea is perfect. You must constantly consider the pros and cons of your ideas and your actions in order to improve yourself as a leader. This will allow only minimal room for error, and ensure that the decisions you make are always well thought out and precise. A successful leader is someone that a strict regime of self-criticism and evaluation in the name of self-improvement.

Self-evaluation is also a useful skill when it comes to dealing with others. If you approach someone with a solid plan that you have already put through a revision process, they will know that your decisions are concrete, and they will understand that you have put your best efforts into helping them with their problem, making you a better leader in their eyes. Furthermore, if you are constantly evaluating yourself then other people will see that you are constantly improving your methods, and you will be known as a better leader for it. As mentioned before, remember that it is beneficial to present others with big ideas, and you should not be apprehensive to do so. The bigger you think, the bigger the opposition will be to your ideas, but this is not a bad thing. If you are constantly evaluating your own ideas, you will know that any opposition to your ideas is unfounded, and simply a result of the misunderstanding of others. You must know that the people you deal with are not big thinkers like you—they are small thinkers, and you need to be able to use the leadership qualities you possess to make them understand the benefits of your ideas, despite any concerns they may have.

If you have evaluated and re-evaluated your ideas as you should you will know the benefit of these ideas, and the necessity for them to be understood and accepted. Do not be afraid to assert yourself and speak your mind if someone opposes your ideas, because as a leader, you know that your own ideas have been carefully crafted and evaluated again and again. You must be ready to defend your own ideas with clear and concise logic and well-crafted arguments. This will come easily to you as a result of your critiquing and evaluation process.

With time, you will be able to convince these small thinkers of the benefits of your ideas. In order to do this, you must lay out your actions clearly in order to make them understand your thought process. Once they understand, they will start to become sympathetic to your ideas, and they will follow you once again when you make it clear that you are determined to continue despite any struggle along the way that they may pose. When you explain your thought process and show that you have the utmost confidence in your own ideas, you will gain back the confidence of any of those who doubt you.

Another valuable skill that you must learn as a leader is to trust in your intuition. Your intuition, or your gut instinct, is a powerful tool that you should always listen to when it presents itself. You know that you are a leader, so make sure to always listen to the "leader within you" in the face of a problem. Your sense of intuition will improve every time you take on a task that requires you to be a leader, because your experience is one of your most valuable assets. Over time, you will see that your intuition will become more relevant and precise as you put your faith in it. Then, in situations where you may not have time to evaluate your choices and choose the best one, your gut instinct will be a lifesaving tool that you can call upon in these kinds of dire circumstances.

When people criticize, you do not become offended, take the criticism with pride, and listen to them with a positive attitude and an open mind. First, ask them what they would do differently if they were faced with the same situation. As a leader you must diplomatically listen to the ideas presented to you, and decide whether or not they are feasible. This decision will be based upon your past experience and your finely tuned instincts.

If you realize that the criticism is warranted and the other person presents you with good ideas, then you should adopt them and alter your plan to suit them. However, if the ideas do not seem constructive, you are by no means obligated to adopt them. If this is the case, you can simply disregard these ideas if you believe as a leader that your plan is the right one. To discard an idea that is presented to you, simply explain your rationale to the person who gave it to you, and be sure to thank them for their contribution to the project. Do not worry if they seem disgruntled—you will have handled the situation as best you could, and they will come around and follow you soon enough.

In my personal experience, it is apparent that most of the people who produce criticism in a group are simply trying to be heard. As a leader, you are by no means above those who look up to you, because a leader that ignores their followers is not a leader at all. If someone approaches you one-on-one and reaches out to you with advice or input on a plan, then you must keep an open mind and listen to them earnestly. If someone reaches out to you in this way, they are not doing it for attention they are doing it because they believe they have good ideas and they want to share them with you. This shows that they care about your opinion and they share your passion for the task at hand.

If other people come to you in this way, you must hold them in high esteem, whether or not you choose to accept their input. These kinds of people are your real followers, and you must realize when these kinds of people present themselves to you. They are valuable assets to you as a leader; they are your true followers, and you should include them in your plans. As a leader, you should covet these individuals and keep them as your "Generals", because you know that you can trust them to produce good ideas and constructive criticism, and you know that they believe in you. You will be their leader, or their "Commander", and together you will become a driving force that can solve any problem that appears before you.

Once you come up with a big idea and have a blueprint to implement it as a result of rigorous evaluation, then it is important to build your own confidence in yourself and in your idea. Most of this confidence will be gained through positive reinforcement as a result of your self-evaluation. Once you are confident in your idea, you have the ability to present it to those around you with a clear vision. With confidence, your presentation will be delivered with conviction and passion, and it will be easier to talk about your idea when you know there are no flaws or gaps in your plan. Furthermore, you will have the ability to easily address any questions that may be presented to you, because you will know your plan inside and out.

While you are presenting your ideas to others, do not allow anyone else to interrupt until you are finished. You must simply lay everything out for others to take in and understand, and then ask for questions or feedback after your presentation. This is a key point because if you allow interruptions during your presentation, it will be seen as a sign of weakness or a lack of confidence by those to whom you are presenting. It is important to avoid negative judgments like this during your presentation because you want your idea to be presented in the best light possible in order for it to be accepted without doubt or delay.

During your presentation, you must speak simply and directly to your audience. A good way to make sure that you are simple and direct is to practice your presentation out loud to yourself or to a friend or family member in order to familiarize yourself with the words you will use. This not only strengthens your delivery but also opens up your presentation for feedback and constructive criticism. If you can confidently present your ideas in a simple and concise manner to your peers, it will easily allow everyone to understand your vision for the plan. When everyone understands your plan and they approve of it, they will be happy to endorse your vision. Each successful presentation will provide you with new opportunities, and each time you successfully carry out a plan you will gain more loyal followers.

Mahatma Gandhi was a simple man who lived a simple life and yet, when he took a small step with a plan in mind, he started a revolution. He did not hesitate to put his plan into action because he knew he had a great vision that would change his entire country for the better. He had the confidence to carry out his plan, and because of this, people began to follow him and idolize him.

Gandhi led the march against the British government in India, and every Indian for miles around came to join with him. Everyone had their reasons for following him but the overarching attraction, and the reason why he gained so many followers, was because he led with purpose and a clear destination in mind. Gandhi understood the pain that Indians felt, and he skillfully used that pain as an advantage against the British government to draw his people together in their support of his goal: freedom for all Indians. These people were loyal followers, and every one of them aided Gandhi in making his vision into a reality. Gandhi undoubtedly faced many roadblocks along the way regardless of his clear vision and his loyal followers. However much he was set back, he persevered and managed to achieve his goal and create a legacy. Despite being beaten, arrested, and thrown in jail, he never gave up until he achieved the goal he set out to reach. This kind of dedication and perseverance is what made Gandhi a true leader.

Chapter 3

Set High Standards, Be Uncomfortable

In this chapter, you will first learn to focus on setting your standards high, and not settling for anything less than the best. Setting high standards for yourself and keeping to them is a crucial step in becoming a strong leader as it will give you room to grow and improve while impressing others with your dedication. The second part of this process, which goes hand in hand with setting high standards, is learning to live outside of your comfort zone. This is a necessary skill to acquire; you will find yourself making slow progress as a leader if you only stick to tasks which you are comfortable carrying out. This chapter will teach you how to push your own boundaries, and become a stronger leader because of it.

In the previous chapter you learned how to think big and produce great, unique ideas that you can present to people in a concise manner. Thinking big is a very small aspect of setting your standards high on a broader scale. As a leader you must set yourself to the highest standards and keep them, and you will continue to grow and develop. Setting your standards high can be a difficult and daunting premise, but it is an essential step in your journey to becoming a successful leader.

Even if you believe you hold high standards for yourself at the current moment, these standards are not high enough if you want to grow and progress in your leadership role. It may be easier to envision when you can think of it in terms of something relatable, such as a school grading system, as this will clearly outline what it is you must do.

In a school grading system your work is assessed objectively by predetermined criteria and, when it is judged, you are provided with a letter grade ranging from 'A' – 'F'. In this grading system an 'A' represents a perfect piece of work, and is the highest grade that you can possibly receive. Conversely, an 'F' grade represents a failing grade, and it is the lowest grade that you can possibly receive – it is usually only given out if the work is incomplete or displays minimal knowledge of the subject matter. In between the 'A' and the 'F' you can receive a 'D', a 'C', or a 'B' for various levels of prowess in the subject matter, increasing as the letters get closer to 'A'.

At the current moment, I believe it is reasonable in this scenario to rule out the possibility that you have set your personal standards to accepting an 'F' as a reasonable grade for your work, as this is a failing grade and shows little or no competence in your field. Perhaps for those who hold themselves in lower esteem, a 'B' would be acceptable, as it is close to a perfect grade and reflects that your work has been done with quite a high level of prowess. Chances are though, that if you are reading this book, you will have set your standards to only accepting an 'A' grade from your work because you want it to be perfect.

Setting your standards to only accepting 'A' grades is the quality of a leader however, if you want to continue to grow and progress as a leader and an individual you must shoot even higher than that. An 'A' grade theoretically represents a perfect piece of work but, upon closer examination, it can be seen that you can receive an 'A' grade for something that is not perfect, so long as it surpasses the requirements for receiving a 'B'. Envisioning yourself in the top percentile of the 'A' grade for your work is the first step in the process of raising your expectations in order to become a true leader.

As a leader, not only do you want to aim to achieve perfection in your endeavors, you want to aim to surpass the qualities that you assume are encompassed within the concept of perfection. In essence, you must hold expectations of yourself that are limitless; you must aim to achieve higher than an 'A' grade by disregarding that system altogether and imagining yourself constantly improving and rising towards a level of perfection that you and others cannot even fathom. It is only in this sense that you will be able to set high enough standards for yourself to allow progression in your journey to become a successful leader.

Once you have achieved a new heightened set of standards for yourself you will likely start to feel uncomfortable. Do not fear, this is a normal reaction to the process, as it is difficult to even describe these new heights you are trying to reach. It is normal to feel uncomfortable because this is the test of a true leader – if you can keep yourself to these heightened standards then it shows that you are worthy to progress in a leadership role and reflects on your strength as an individual.

This sense of discomfort produced by the standards you set for yourself as a leader is a powerful force which you must learn to harness. If you are uncomfortable, you will do everything in your power to make yourself feel comfortable again. It is important that you harness this potential to raise yourself up to meet your heightened standards. Once you realize that you can continue to improve yourself as a leader by setting continually higher standards, you will live in a scenario where there is only one option. In order to ease your discomfort, you must improve yourself and, in doing this, you will find peace and a sense of accomplishment.

When you feel a sense of unease, it means you have breached the boundaries of your comfort zone. Breaking out of your comfort zone is a positive thing, as it will open you up to the possibility of new experiences, and it shows that you are growing as a leader. Your comfort zone, while you may be inclined to stay inside of it, is simply a barrier between you and the achievement of true leadership. Your comfort zone holds you back in your journey to becoming a successful leader because it does not allow for growth and progress, and as such, it must be traversed.

It is vital to use your heightened set of self-standards to expand beyond your comfort zone, as it is a quality that is possessed by true leaders. You must always feel and foster that sensation of having butterflies in your stomach, because it keeps you on your toes and ensures that you always perform to the best of your abilities when you are under pressure. Remember though that it is very important to remain in control of the situation and, most importantly, yourself.

Existing outside of your comfort zone is essential to your growth as a leader, but you must remember to never let yourself be overwhelmed. If this happens you will enter the "panic zone", a space in your mind that you could occupy in order to feel safe in the face of a bombardment of new and overly-stimulating experiences. Do not allow yourself to enter the panic zone, as this will lead to distraction and loss of direction. If you begin to feel overwhelmed, simply remind yourself that you are a leader and believe in yourself, and you will find that you can tackle any obstacle.

This delicate path that you must walk while you remain outside of your comfort zone is much like walking on a tightrope. You must maintain the feeling of danger by existing outside of your comfort zone and, simultaneously, you must know that you need to be focused and fully in control to reach the other side of the rope. Like walking on a tightrope, the achievements that you reach outside of your comfort zone will provide you with satisfaction and fulfillment, and will open you up for future challenges and uncomfortable experiences as a leader.

In order to combat the feeling of danger or discomfort that arises from existing outside of your comfort zone, you must envision your goal and the satisfaction you will gain from reaching it. As a leader, you must learn to thrive in an uncomfortable environment and enjoy every moment and every step you take, because you know that it is bringing you ever closer to the success you desire. Once you attain success you will truly realize the necessity of existing outside of your comfort zone, even if it feels unnatural and overwhelming. The bottom line is that you must always keep your goal in mind, and this is how you will remain motivated and content; this is what will give you the ability to keep going.

This is an essential skill that all successful leaders must possess; you must be able to channel your emotions into a means of motivation. You must learn to focus in on the happy thoughts that you have when you think of reaching your goal, and these emotions will fuel your passion.

Happy thoughts are more powerful than any negative emotions so, as a leader, you must train yourself to always keep these positive thoughts in mind. This will make you more productive and it will spur your growth as an individual and as a leader.

On top of cultivating your own positive thoughts and emotions, you must also consider the emotions of those around you. If you do great things, and you continue to push yourself, people will admire you and follow you. If they witness your great actions, especially if you provide help to them specifically, they will radiate happiness and thankfulness for your presence in their lives. They will feel satisfied and grateful for your abilities and, due to the positive emotions emanating from your followers, you will be lifted up even higher than you were before, and you will be known as a strong and successful leader.

If you combine the happiness that you provide for others with the self-satisfaction you gain from reaching your goals, it will create a helpful channel that spawns success and the possibility of your endeavors in the future. You can almost condition yourself in this way; train yourself to imagine the outcomes of your actions if you reach your goal and all the internal and external happiness you will create then you will find it significantly easier to succeed.

Now that you have learned how to heighten your self-standards and to live outside your comfort zone, and you have understood the benefits of these practices, you will learn some tips to cope with the pressure of this demanding lifestyle. As we have established, it feels natural and good to stay within the bounds of your comfort zone. However, as a leader, you know that life is not that simple, and that you must traverse the outer reaches of your comfort zone on the journey to success. Thus, you must know how to deal with this harsh and uncomfortable reality of leadership.

As previously noted, you must utilize happy and positive emotions from yourself and those around you to decrease the discomfort that is an unfortunate by-product of existing outside of your comfort zone. Thus, whenever you hit the edge of your comfort zone, you must bring happier moments to the forefront of your mind in order to ease your temperament. Over time this prevailing sense of unease will begin to take a toll, which is why it is useful to learn a new way of thinking about your comfort zone.

Think of your comfort zone as a literal circle around your body, with you in the exact center of the circle. At the beginning of your journey to becoming a successful leader this circle was likely quite small and close to your body, because your comfort zone was narrow. You were unable or unwilling to open yourself up to experiences that made you feel uncomfortable, of which there were a lot, which is why the circle of your comfort zone was small like everyone else's.

Now, as a leader, all of your experiences throughout your journey to success have culminated to increase your comfort zone, as you have been subjected to new experiences that may have caused apprehension. Thus, if we think of your comfort zone as a circle, it has expanded as a result of all of these new experiences. When you reach the edge of your comfort zone, you must utilize your happy thoughts like a beacon in the darkness to further widen the circle of light around you.

If you successfully adopt this method, you can increase your comfort zone indefinitely by simply keeping a positive attitude in the face of your unease. Think of the circle of your comfort zone as your kingdom, while you the leader are the king in charge of it. A good king does not sit back and rule a small patch of land; rather, he explores the limits of his kingdom and constantly makes an effort to expand it for the good of himself and his people. When you learn to control your comfort zone, you will be in control of your own potential to succeed.

Over time, by using this technique, your comfort zone will continue to grow into a very large circle based on all of your successes and your continued growth as a leader. You will be able to reflect with pride upon all of the things that are within your comfort zone now that were never there at the start of your journey to become a successful leader. This is by no means an absolute victory because, as a leader, you should constantly attempt to expand your comfort zone to new areas. This technique is meant as more of a checkpoint to aid you in reaching your next objective; a marker of your progress to assure that you do not lose your way.

The purpose of all this, and the main thing you should gain from these explanations, is that the feeling of unease that will become commonplace to you is actually a good thing. You can harness this unease to motivate yourself and increase your comfort zone, and above all, unease is a sign that you are on the right path. Each time you feel your heart skip a few beats due to the stress of a new and frightening situation, you can take solace in the fact that this feeling is incredibly useful. You must know that when you feel uncomfortable in the face of a new experience it is not a sign of weakness. Rather, this feeling is entirely normal and it is a sign that you are growing as a leader.

As a leader you must know that it is necessary to take risks in order to achieve success in your journey. Personal happiness and fulfillment are not reached simply by the action of taking a risk, but taking risks will often aid you in your endeavors on a smaller scale. It is a fact that you will need to take some risks throughout your journey in order to reach your goals. Reaching your goals is always a successful achievement, and having the confidence to take risks to get closer to these goals is a vital skill that you must possess.

Like most of the leadership practices, you will learn that taking risks becomes easier over time. It can be quite hard to take that first leap but, as a leader, you must find the courage within yourself to do so. Make sure to remember that every time you take a risk, you are making a calculated decision to get you closer to your goal of success.

Furthermore, other people will admire your ability to take risks as a leader if you perfect this technique. Every time you take a risk, they will realize that you are taking that risk in place of them, and they will feel grateful for it. People will admire you for your selfless efforts, and this will produce more loyal followers to aid you in your journey.

To be a successful leader that stands the test of time, you must be able to master the essential leadership qualities that have been outlined earlier in this chapter. Think of this process like building a tower by stacking individual blocks on top of each other. As a leader you are this tower—a strong and large structure that people will look up to. Like building a tower, when it comes to learning and instilling the qualities of a leader, you must start simple and work your way up.

You started your journey with the earlier chapters of this book, and each skill that you set out to learn was expanded upon and realized in the increasingly more complex skills with which you were presented as you continued to read. Thus, the first skill you learned from this book was the first building block in your tower of leadership, and every other skill since then has built itself on top of the other skills you have learned.

As you continue to progress as a leader, your tower of skills will continue to build itself higher and higher until eventually you are able to reach your goals and attain success.

Thinking of your leadership skills in this unique way is a useful technique as it allows you to reflect on yourself as a leader. If you can visualize how high your tower of leadership has become, and all of the individual blocks within it, then you will be able to see your progress as a leader. The more blocks there are in your tower, the more progress you have made towards reaching your goals. Your loyal followers will also be able to realize your progress in their own ways, and they will support you and admire you for all of your effort and hard work.

All successful leaders throughout history have proven that they started out with a clear vision. The true test of leadership that was passed by all great leaders is the ability to stay focused on that vision. These leaders have shown great courage and perseverance in the battle to reach their goals. More importantly they have shown that they could not be brought down by any of the many hardships they came into contact with; rather, they faced these hardships head-on and endured.

Furthermore, all of the notable leaders of the world have always valued their purpose above their own personal feelings. The mark of a true leader is to keep your eyes on the prize, regardless of how it makes you feel as an individual. If times are hard, you must remind yourself of the goal and the benefits that you and those around you will capitalize on once your goal is reached.

The ability of these famous figures to place faith in their purpose above their feelings is what ultimately made them successful. Do you think a leader such as Mahatma Gandhi reached his goals without feeling downtrodden and disgruntled at times? The answer is no, but you must realize that in order to reach his goals Gandhi put his vision at the forefront of his efforts, and forgot about his own personal troubles in the name of a noble cause for the Indian people.

Take Abraham Lincoln, for example. Lincoln was a great leader and became the sixteenth president of the United States as a result of his continued efforts. Lincoln is a prime example of a self-built individual, as he started from nothing and built his own legacy. Take Lincoln's story into account if you begin to feel unsatisfied with your progress, and use it as inspiration to continue your journey to becoming a successful leader like him.

Abraham Lincoln started out as a simple farm boy, born in Kentucky, and was largely self-educated. This process of self-education marked the beginning of Lincoln's journey to becoming a leader, as he took his future into his own hands. He was not going to settle for living as a poor farmer for the rest of his days; instead, he decided he wanted to make a name for himself.

As a result of Lincoln's self-education, he managed to become a lawyer in Illinois, and served for many years as a member of government there. He then managed to move up the ranks, as he gained more skill in his field, and was eventually elected to the United States House of Representatives. This new position gave him a level of power and success that he had never dreamed of when he was still living as a farm boy in Kentucky, and he used his new-found success to greatly improve the United States economy with his ambitious vision.

After serving for a while in this position Lincoln became aware that the voters in his area largely disagreed with some of his views, which prompted his return to practicing law. Feeling defeated is a natural part of any journey to become a successful leader, and Lincoln is only human like the rest of us. He became disgruntled when he felt like he could progress no further in politics, and so he began to practice law once again, a step down in the ranks of leadership.

Because Lincoln is a true leader, he later managed to muster the courage and dedication to re-enter the political field and pursue his path to success once again. He became a leading figure in the new Republican Party, and battled against other politicians for years in order to have his voice heard. As a result of his continued efforts, Lincoln was eventually elected president of the United States.

Lincoln was elected president likely because of the peoples' faith in his progressive views. He was not afraid to stay true to his beliefs and, like a true leader, he pressed on and managed to convince the majority to put their faith in him and his abilities. However, he faced great backlash for his opinions in some of the Southern states, due to his views against slavery, which caused great tension in the nation and eventually led to the American Civil War.

It takes a true leader to continue on the path that is right in the face of such conflict as the civil war, and Lincoln proved himself to be the leader the people needed. He knew that slavery must be abolished, and he selflessly guided his nation through a civil war in order to see his views become a reality. Lincoln oversaw many policies that were quite controversial at the time, but it led to justice when he ended the war and produced the Emancipation Proclamation in an effort to combat slavery.

Eventually, he saw the Thirteenth Amendment to the United States Constitution passed through congress, which permanently outlawed slavery across the nation.

As you can see by Lincoln's story, the world needs true leaders in order to progress. In order to be the leader you desire to be you must always keep your goal in mind and never back down for anything once you know it is the right thing to do. Lincoln's story also shows us that it is possible, through perseverance and dedication, to make yourself into a great leader from nothing, solely through your own efforts.

Lincoln's beliefs were considered controversial by many, but he pressed on because he knew it was in the name of justice. When people realized his passion and his determination, they began to follow him and lift him up as a great leader. Lincoln's passion and effort, and his refusal to give up on what he believed in, were the qualities that made him a successful leader. Through his role as a leader, Lincoln was able to change the world for the better.

Chapter 4

Be Practical, Logical, and Tough

In this chapter you will learn the importance of self-discipline, and the need to be practical and logical in your plans. Building on the previous chapter, you will now learn to become a leader with the ability to truly catalyze change. Learning this ability will cause more people to follow you because they will believe in your potential to direct meaningful change in their lives. Your followers are one of your biggest areas of strength as a leader thus you must learn how to put their needs above your own. The greater good is the cause that you must fight for as a strong leader; self-improvement will come as a by-product of your courageous efforts to change the lives of those around you. This chapter will teach you how to maintain a necessary level of discipline as a leader, and how to remain selfless.

All good leaders must, above all, be practical in everything they do, ranging from their daily tasks, to helping others, and to setting practical and achievable goals. Therefore, as a leader you must learn to hold practicality in high esteem. As a leader you do not imagine spending a lot of time in an effort to achieve something that serves no purpose other than being stylish. Rather, you must set goals for yourself that only account for the necessities. This is because you will be faced with a lot of responsibilities at once, all of which you must tend to in order to be seen as a strong leader.

In the hopes of becoming a more practical individual, you must think of things objectively and without bias. If you start to favour certain tasks over others, you are thinking subjectively which will lead to the draining of valuable resources and an overall waste of your time that is better spent in other ways. Practicality becomes most necessary in the planning stages of your projects, but this is not to say that practicality will be useless at other times. Being practical is a necessary skill that you must possess if you wish to be a successful leader as it will ensure that you stick to your plan and keep on track to your destination.

A good example of practicality is as follows. If you are commissioned to build a brick wall with a team of workers, you must attempt to carry out this project in the least amount of time possible while still achieving the desired results. In order to do this you must plan to be practical. When you are picking your team of workers you may have the option to choose between one of your friends and someone that you do not necessarily get along with. The catch here is that your friend is not as skilled a worker as the other person.

In this case, the practical decision would be to choose the person that is the better worker. Even though you could have chosen your friend, and they would have raised morale in the group due to your closeness, you must be objective and choose the person that you are not friends with. This is because you know that the better worker will help you to get the job done faster, and in a more professional manner. The ability to make objective decisions like this is what separates you as a leader from the rest of the people around you.

However, if it were the case that the person you do not necessarily get along with holds some hostility towards you, it would be another matter. In that case, the more practical decision would be to choose your friend. This is because the other worker, while they are more proficient than your friend, would cause a toxic work environment. Hostility in the workplace will lower productivity and create unnecessary roadblocks, which is why the practical decision in this scenario would be to choose your friend to be a member of your team.

As you can see, being practical is all about assessing the situation at hand and deciding what your best course of action will be. Practicality is an essential skill to learn in your journey to becoming a successful leader because the ability to be practical will ensure that your time is well-spent and that your goals are achieved. This leadership technique will take some time to get used to but do not be discouraged. With effort you will succeed and, if you continue to practice being a practical individual, you will see that it will pay off. Honing your ability to be practical will cause people to admire you because this is a difficult and well-sought-after skill to learn. People are usually not thinking practically in their everyday lives because they succumb to their individual needs and feelings, but this is what separates you from them as a leader.

Existing hand in hand with practicality is the ability to be logical. As a leader you must remain logical at all times, without giving in to your wants and needs if they will sway you from the correct path. In the scenario mentioned above where you are commissioned to build a brick wall, it would be useful to remain logical in both your decisions and your actions. If you chose the better worker to be a part of your team, you as a leader would know it to be the logical choice. You would then have to logically and plainly explain to your friend that there are no hard feelings, but the other worker was the more practical choice for the job.

If you are not logical you will find yourself in the realm of indecisiveness, which may lead to panic. This will cause a halt in your productivity, and a halt in your growth as a leader, so you should attempt to avoid this at all costs. Every problem and every scenario has a logical solution, and you have the ability to discern it. If you are ever feeling like logic escapes you, you should remedy the situation before making any rash decisions that you may later regret. A good night's sleep is always a much-needed remedy if you are feeling unsure in your own ability to remain logical. As a leader you must always be at your best, and in order to do that, you must know when to give your body the rest it needs and deserves. This is not a sign of weakness but a sign of wisdom. A true leader knows and accepts when they are not performing at their best, and does everything in their power to remedy it.

To bring these concepts of logic and practicality together, as a leader, you must be specific, and give clear directions to those working with you. Do not give vague instructions to other workers as this will leave room for error and misinterpretation. As a leader you must consider all of the possible outcomes, and account for any negative ones where the project does not meet the standards you have set for it.

This is why it is so important, as is mentioned in previous chapters, to have a clear vision before you set out to work on a project. If you have a clear vision, and you have subjected your plan to rigorous evaluation, you will know exactly what needs to be done to reach your goal. Thus, you will be able to give clear and precise instructions to those working with you that will allow the project to run smoothly and without confusion or delay.

Having the ability to be logical, practical, and specific all at the same time is the mark of a true leader. This will allow you to adequately measure any situation because these three skills are the cornerstones of any problem that needs to be solved. Once you are able to use these skills adequately, you will be able to achieve the goals you desire much more easily. Having the ability to measure any given situation and pinpoint the solution to any problem is an extremely useful skill as a leader, and you will find it necessary in many aspects of your life.

Another benefit that comes from being able to expertly measure any given situation is that you will receive notoriety for it. In order to be a successful leader you must be realistic, yet optimistic in all situations with which you are faced. This will demonstrate to others that you truly know what you are doing, while also giving them hope and something to look forward to with the promise of reaching your goal. In this way, you will be trusted as a leader to truly want what it is that you desire, and people will follow you because they know you will be the person they need to produce clear and beneficial results in their lives.

It is a fact that a leader who wants to see change, like Abraham Lincoln, is a leader that people will want to follow forever. People desire positive change, and you should aim to be the kind of leader who can give it to them. The support of the people is paramount to your success as a leader, so you must focus on the changes that people want to see in the world, and you will be on a sure-fire path to success in a leadership role. If you succeed in becoming a leader that can produce positive change in the world in the eyes of others, your followers will view you as a "transformative individual." This means that they put their faith in you, and they believe in your ability to transform the world around you to make it a more positive space.

To ensure that the people around you hold you in high esteem, you must assess their problems one-on-one and show them that you truly care for their well-being. Meeting with the members of your community is an essential part of your job as a great leader, and you should not take this responsibility lightly. Make sure to keep in touch with all of your followers and the people around you in order to maintain a good relationship with them. This will be mutually beneficial as you will provide them with aid and the promise of change, and in return you will gain their support.

Next, you must evaluate your concept of progress as a leader. In previous chapters it has been noted that you will receive satisfaction and the feeling of personal growth from your experiences as a leader. However, it is clear that most leaders wish to see notable signs of progress in their own life as a result of becoming a leader. These signs of progress can be things such as money, fame, or power, which most leaders will likely want to achieve in their lives.

However, it is important to see things like money, fame, and power for what they truly are. These are wonderful things, and they are fitting rewards for your leadership but these are not what you should be aiming for in your journey to become a successful leader. These are shallow goals, and should only be accepted as a by-product of your true goals. A true leader will realize that possessions and importance on an individual scale are merely stepping stones along the path to their true destination.

One of the most important values you must instill in yourself as a leader is to avoid placing too much emphasis on the by-products of your success. Things like money, fame, and power are nice but if these are your ultimate goals then you are not a true leader at all. A great leader is someone who places the majority of their efforts into an emphasis on helping others.

If you cultivate a passion for helping others you will understand the multitude of benefits it provides. In addition to rewarding you with by products like worldly possessions and prestige, helping those around you will provide you with a profound sense of accomplishment and satisfaction that cannot be obtained through other means. As a leader helping others to succeed is what truly makes you great because you will be sowing a sustainable future for future generations. If you focus on the positive change that others want to see in the world, then you will truly be on the path to enlightenment and success in a leadership role.

A true leader not only helps others to succeed but actively places the needs of others before the needs of themselves. This is a quality that you must learn if you wish to become a great leader. Putting the needs of others before your own needs will show those around you that you are a selfless leader, which is an admirable quality. This will show people that you care deeply about them, and it will ensure that your followers are loyal and devoted, and that they believe in your abilities to succeed and create a positive change in the world.

Having loyal followers is a very valuable asset as a leader, and you must learn to cultivate relationships with those around you because of it. You must learn to use your decisions and your actions to empower those around you. If they know that you hold their needs above your own, then your actions and decisions will represent your dedication to them, and they will remain loyal to you in order to express their gratitude.

Until now, when you have learned about maintaining relationships with your peers and cultivating a group of loyal followers, it may have seemed extravagant and even a little unnecessary. Perhaps you asked yourself why you would need followers to help you grow as a leader if the ultimate means of achieving your goals still rests on your shoulders.

Sure, there are many benefits to having followers but it may seem as if your time would be better spent growing your own leadership capabilities. This is entirely a falsehood. Loyal followers are undoubtedly helpful to your cause in many ways but you must now learn the main reason why cultivating followers is so important in your journey to becoming a successful leader. When you have built a loyal group of people that are grateful and devoted to you because of your leadership, the next step for these followers is empowerment—and you are the figure they need in order to achieve it.

As a leader you must use your actions and decisions to empower those around you so that they can become leaders in their own right. This is one of the most important responsibilities you will have as a leader.

You must stand alone as a role model to your followers and, through your actions, you must learn to empower them and mold them into future leaders so that they can follow in your footsteps. This will be the essence of your legacy, and will leave behind a sustainable system that will continue to aid others for many years to come.

Now, we must retrace our steps to the anecdote about the brick wall in order to illustrate the essence of a great leader's mindset. This story will help you visualize what it means to think and exist like a true leader, and how you must inspire the people around you to heighten their ambitions and strive for greatness like you.

Imagine three men laying bricks, as they have been commissioned to build a brick wall, and they are working together to complete the project. These three men are going about their business, all working to the best of their abilities, when they notice another man walking towards them. This passerby stops and admires the wall and the handiwork of the men, and takes a minute to consider what is before him. He then asks the three men a seemingly simple question: "what are you doing?"

The first man, a good, professional construction worker that excels in his field, replies to the passerby by saying "I am making a living."

This man goes on to say that he is working for his father in hopes of inheriting the family construction business. His father is a reasonable man, but he believes that his son should learn the trade before he can manage it, and so this man is giving his best effort to learning the necessary skills required to take over his father's business. This man clearly has some incentive to give his all to building the brick wall, but he is not a true leader; he has not set his sights high enough and his goals are limiting in nature.

The second man, a more cynical individual, gives a literal response to the passerby by saying "I am laying bricks." This man goes on to say that he is simply trying to make ends meet, and so he has been working part-time as a construction worker for the past few years. He is clearly proficient at the work that he is providing for the company by laying bricks for the wall, but he ultimately lacks ambition. This man has no goal in life aside from the simple wish to get by. This man is even less of a true leader than the first man in this respect, as he is not even fully in control of his own life, and he does not possess a competitive attitude that is required to make a meaningful difference.

The third man, having listened to the replies of his companions before him, sits back from his work for a minute and seems to ponder the question, and consider the answers that were already given. The man then turns to the passerby and says "I am building a library where hundreds of people will gain the necessary knowledge to become leaders." This third man perfectly exemplifies the way that a true leader must think of all that he does. Even a simple and seemingly meaningless task such as brick-laying can provide a significant outcome for a great leader.

As a leader you must exemplify the thought process and the mindset of the third man in this scenario. You must take all of the valuable lessons you have learned thus far and culminate them into a personal checklist that will aid you in your journey to become a successful leader. Much like the third man, you must foster big dreams and high expectations, and you will find meaning and passion in the seemingly less significant tasks that you are responsible for. Furthermore, this man's big dreams will likely inspire his co-workers to aspire to become something greater as well.

Gary Burnison, the CEO of a top executive search company called Korn Ferry, provides some advice to aspiring leaders in his book entitled *The Leadership Journey*. In this book Burnison writes, "develop the ability to lead yourself by first acknowledging your strengths and weaknesses." With these words Burnison reminds us that in order to be a leader for others, we must first be sure to lead ourselves.

Assessing and realizing your strengths and weaknesses is a valuable skill that you must possess in order to be a successful leader. It is the quality of a true leader to be able to admit your own strengths and weaknesses, because it shows that you are proud of your abilities and you know exactly who you are and what your potential is for success in different areas. Realizing your strengths and weaknesses will not only improve your quality as a leader, but it will improve your life as an individual and it will allow you to fully know yourself.

Burnison's quote also reminds us of the importance of constant self-assessment in the quest to be a successful leader. As you have learned earlier, self-evaluation and constructive criticism are essential leadership skills, and they provide a multitude of benefits that will allow you to grow as a leader and as an individual. Self-assessment will effectively allow you to acknowledge your own strengths and weaknesses through the process of self-reflection.

This practice of self-evaluation and self-reflection is a very important step in your journey to becoming a successful leader, as you likely understand by now. The main benefit of it, aside from self-improvement, is that it will serve to remind you of your full potential as a leader. When you reflect you must simultaneously look forward to the future and imagine what you can become as a result of this intimate knowledge of yourself. As a result of confronting your potential you will be given the ability to create visions bigger than you ever could have imagined, and your potential and your success as a leader will only continue to grow.

In order to better understand the idea of self-discipline and, the benefit of inspiring your followers, we turn to the great historical leader Genghis Khan, who unified the previously sparse and warring tribes of Mongolia under one flag and managed to rule them all himself. Genghis, as dictated by the culture of his people at the time, stuck to an extreme regimen of self-discipline even as a boy. After his father's death he was challenged to survive harsh weather conditions and a life of poverty until he managed to become wise and strong enough to form a plan. Genghis's survival was all due to the strong resolve he possessed, he had a leader's capabilities even from a young age. His vision was to unite the unorganized tribes of Mongolia and to lead them himself in conquest across the lands. To reach his position as the newly proclaimed 'Khan' of the Mongolian people, he endured many hardships and roadblocks along the way which he was able to overcome.

This is because he kept his focus on achieving his goals before anything else. Genghis Khan was an incredibly inspiring leader for his people because he managed to build a powerful nation out of what was essentially nothing. His followers were loyal, and they believed in him because he had proven himself to be a great leader that brought positive change to the Mongolian people. The sheer loyalty of Genghis's followers was one of his strongest attributes as a leader. Genghis could not have harnessed the power of his followers if he did not possess the qualities of a strong leader, but his people were an essential element in the formation of the nation which he ruled over.

With his extremely loyal followers, Genghis was able to build a legacy that lasted for many generations. All of the systems he put in place were handed down and built upon to be improved over time, but it is important to note that he alone made the blueprints for this vision. After his death the followers which he had cultivated were inspired and empowered by his leadership, and they continued in his footsteps. Many other Khans ruled in Genghis's place after he was gone, and this is because Genghis was able to form close relationships with his people and make them into leaders of their own.

You must take the principles you learned in this chapter, such as self-discipline and the ability to empower your followers, and instill them as values in your life. Take Genghis's story of creating something from nothing, and use it as an inspiration to improve yourself and to continue your journey to become a more successful leader. If you do this you will continue to grow and progress as a leader and you will successfully begin to build your legacy.

Chapter 5

Be Enthusiastic and Expressive

In the previous chapter, we spoke at length as to how a true leader can outwardly influence those around him with his practicality and with reason. These visible marks of a determined leader will be something that we will touch on again throughout this book, but in this chapter we will look more inwards at the thoughts which you direct not at others, but upon yourself, and the impact that this can have on how your progress.

One of the lessons which I have learned over my years was the value of not just how I outwardly showed those close to me how much they meant, but also how valuable it was to love myself in the process. Our minds can be fickle beasts at times; one minute they are our most valuable asset, forging in us a determination to make the world a better place, and the next they focus on our insecurities and fears, hindering our ability to improve.

As all of you reading this book will undoubtedly know, when you are feeling fulfilled and like you are moving in the right direction, this can snowball into a wave of productivity and success, as you apply your optimism to all areas of your life. Each of us has had a day where we start on the right foot, and the morning goes so well that you lunge into the afternoon with gusto and pride and accomplish that which you wanted to complete in the day. And of course, on the other side of the coin, we have all had days where we wake up feeling like today is just not our day. The morning's negativity can then flow into our afternoon and into the evening, leaving us feeling unfulfilled and disappointed in ourselves.

This is why being able to love and forgive yourself is so important. When times are good, it is easy to think highly of yourself and to carry this energy into the next activity. It is when times are tougher that you must dig deeper into that resolve and say internally and with sincerity, "I love you and I forgive you." When you fall and make mistakes along the way, forgive yourself. When times are tough and you did not manage to quite succeed, forgive yourself. And when you are unsure if you have made the right decision in the past, forgive and love yourself all the same because you have grown throughout the process. None of us have lived a perfect life, nor have we made every decision along our path the right one. The most important part, though, is to remember that it's ok.

We are all on a journey along the path to becoming the leaders we all can be. Along the way, as I have said before, there will be many challenges that harden your resolve and cause you to dig deep for the inner strength needed to forge ahead. This resilience is what I have pushed during the last few chapters, but in the process of acquiring this resilience, do not allow yourself to become cold and uncaring. A true leader knows that not only his or her outward actions shape our selves but also our inward thoughts and reflections. Being able to love and forgive yourself will help you weather the days of struggle and hardship when you would rather not face the world anymore, because you know that tomorrow will come anew. The challenges of becoming a leader will still be there in the morning and you must strengthen your resolve to face them. However, this choice will become easier the more you love yourself throughout your journey. Believe me when I say that if you are able to forgive yourself for the inevitable stumbles which we all encounter, you will progress faster and further than you can believe to be possible.

It is a skill that not enough of us possess to be able to sit at the end of the day and to truly evaluate our successes and forgive our failures. But in the process of this self-reflection, you can learn so much more about yourself than any teacher could tell you. Everyone will have a different way they find to be most beneficial to them when carrying out this self-reflection, but here is one way I have used before. I would sit down in a quiet room before I was about to go to bed, without others talking to me and without distractions such as a TV or computer. I would then go through my day, hour by hour and honestly assess how I had done. In each situation, had I done the best I could? Was I being the best leader I could be in those times? The answer was not always yes. It is easy to reflect on your successes because you are proud of what you accomplished, and you certainly should learn from them. In this case, I would write down how I had done well and how I could use that in the days to come. But I would also critically examine that which I felt I had not accomplished in as successful a manner. Some days, this would be just one thing that had not gone how I wanted it to, and I could draw a lesson from that to try again tomorrow with a new approach. Some days, there would be plenty of mishaps which I had felt I had not handled in the best way possible. These days were the most valuable. Because in each of our failures comes a lesson for future success.

Say, for example, you had a bad day at work and that you were yelled at for something which was not your fault. After work, when you think back on this moment, you can see it either as something that simply happened during your day or you can use it as a lesson to grow. Someone who is unmotivated to grow further will brush it off and ignore it because he knows it was not his fault. A true leader will recognize this as an opportunity for growth. Instead, recognize how you could have handled the situation better, or even to your advantage. Staying quiet and doing nothing to fix the problem will not make you stronger. However, finding out where the confusion lay and why you are being blamed for something could improve not only your work life but that of the workplace around you. By trying to actively fix an issue, you would then move on to be able to enact this change in other parts of your life and grow overall.

Throughout your journey, you will be able to make use of this self-reflection to improve yourself and thus your life around you. In time, this nightly practice of looking back at my day helped me become more self-aware of how I was acting. Instead of living my life on autopilot, I was able to actively consider my actions and to take steps towards fixing the parts which were not benefitting me. The impact over time was such that instead of doing a nightly reflection, I would consider more of what I was doing in the moment and was able to control the negative thoughts which would have served no purpose or helped me move forward. This evaluation helps you stay motivated, as you recognize the differences which can, and do, help shift the mentality of how you become an inspired leader.

This progress did not take long to show itself in my day to day world. I felt empowered and far more in control of different aspects of my life. My relationships with friends and family improved, my colleagues at work noticed a change and, perhaps most important of all, I felt better about myself. As I said before, the impact of your mental state on your ability to improve daily cannot be overstated.

Along the way, I noticed something even more positive; I was feeling more joy in my day to day life. I had been working so hard on improving myself, I had almost forgotten to feel the joy in it! Remember, you are not a machine built to improve. You are flesh and blood and bones and emotion and that is what a leader must recognize; his humanity.

Enjoy the journey! Without having enjoyment and feeling pleasure at your improvement, you will not fully appreciate that which you have accomplished. I have stressed the benefits of reflecting on your actions, but do not do so in a robotic manner. We are often taught that from a young age we must control our emotions, and while we must not let them be unrestrained, I would fully encourage you to embrace them internally.

Feel the sorrow of failure; let that strengthen your resolve to improve tomorrow. And embrace the joy of success and know that you deserve to feel the pride that is welling up within you. Take pride in your accomplishments, and let the knowledge that you have improved take hold within and inspire further action. It is not enough to outwardly improve yourself if you don't feel like you have joy from this. Many individuals will work for years in jobs or careers which they do not like, but in which they strive to improve because of the pressures put on them. There is no shame in their working hard, but material gain is a poor gauge of how successful you will become over time. Not feeling the joy in your journey will leave you a husk, which is why we see so many men and women later on in their lives breaking free from their careers and completely changing direction. They are seeking the joy that was missing from their lives, and this is why I tell you all this now.

Seek the joy in the journey. Embrace it. Love it. Feel like this is the reason you are improving, because I assure you it is possible to see yourself grow in leaps and bounds if you are able to enjoy the route of improvement along which you are travelling. Self-reflection will help you achieve that which you did not believe possible, but enjoying the revelations which it unveils to you will help you so much more. Enjoy the journey, embrace the challenges and you will in time grow to know that you are becoming a truly inspirational leader to those around you.

Chapter 6
Focus on the Next Move

Leadership is the capacity to translate vision into reality. It follows that spontaneous leaders must be forward thinking in their approach to life. They must be able to focus on the outcome. Leaders see more than others see. They see farther than others see. And they see before others see. Their vision is beyond the present. But as mentioned, leadership also takes vision. Great leaders see things as they are and they see how things could be. They help others see what's possible by sharing compelling visions and inspiring others to adopt those visions. Here are leadership quotes on vision (on focusing on the outcome):

Instead of looking at the past, I put myself ahead twenty years and try to look at what I need to do now in order to get there [by] then.
— Diana Ross

The most pathetic person in the world is someone who has sight but no vision.
— Helen Keller

Anybody can look at a pretty girl and see a pretty girl. An artist can look at a pretty girl and see the old woman she will become. A better artist can look at an old woman and see the pretty girl that she used to be. But a great artist —a master—and that is what Auguste Rodin was—can look at

an old woman, portray her exactly as she is . . . and
force the viewer to see the pretty girl she used to be . . .
and more than that, he can make anyone with the sensitivity
of an armadillo, or even you, see that this lovely young girl
is still alive, not old and ugly at all, but simply prisoned
inside her ruined body.
— Robert A. Heinlein, Stranger in a Strange Land

The first step toward creating an improved future is
developing the ability to envision it. VISION will ignite the
fire of passion that fuels our commitment to do WHATEVER
IT TAKES to achieve excellence. Only VISION allows us
to transform dreams of greatness into the reality of achievement
through human action. VISION has no boundaries and
knows no limits. Our VISION is what we become in life.
— Tony Dungy

If you wish to be a great leader, make it your focus to serve those whom you would lead. There are a lot of people who want the power, prestige and pay that comes along with leadership positions but few want to do what it takes to actually be a good and effective leader. Great leadership isn't about bossing people around; it's about inspiring and guiding people towards a common goal for everyone's benefit. It's about inspiring them to focus on the outcome. This can be done by building your team up to where you want them to be, by giving them credit for their work, by praising them for their efforts and by rewarding them when they succeed. There is a saying that states, "Be the change that you want to see." We can adapt that to this discussion by saying, "Be the leader that you would want to lead you."

It is said that there are people who let things happen, people who don't know what's happening, people who don't care what's happening and, most importantly, people who make things happen. Good leaders always look to make things happen through strategy, creativity, focus and energy.

Here are four things leaders do to generate organizational momentum:

1. **Thinking ahead** (focusing on the outcome) creates margin by forecasting probable successes and avoiding potential failures. Thinking ahead also involves challenging old/current processes, equipment, systems, and methodology. Good leaders are always in a constant state of self and organizational evaluation. In other words, leaders don't just live in the moment; they look to the future and lead their organization to get there.

2. Good leaders always **have solid people** around them; they nurture a culture of feedback/ idea generation and provide a safe place for their team members to speak up.

3. Good leaders **take necessary steps** to avoid surprises, lulls, downtime, complacency and inactivity.

4. Leaders always **think strategically** about their people and their future—and the organization and its future. This will give you the edge over your competition and, more importantly, will keep you leading your team into success.

At the basis of every great leader is the ability to develop and nurture relationships between people. Perhaps you've seen this picture: behind three men straining to pull one man sitting on a chair upon a block labeled MISSION. There is an arrow pointing towards the one sitting which says: BOSS. Underneath, there is a second image of all four men pulling the block labeled MISSION. There is no chair. The arrow now points to the man in front, and it says: LEADER. The point? A leader understands that without those supporting him his efforts mean little, as it is through the product of sustained and cooperative effort that the proverbial mission block moves.

A leader is part of a team. She doesn't sit behind and give orders. She works with everybody in order to effectively change the dynamic and outcome of the collective efforts of all involved. This requires an awareness of the contributions and talents of those around you, as well as their limitations and weaknesses. Being able to leverage these skills and weaknesses in such a way that you are able to give proper credit and responsibilities to deserving parties is important, because people are valuable. It's necessary to not only see the value in your coworkers but to express your appreciation of it when it is evident and deserving. When working collaboratively with others it is important for people to be able to see the product of their individual efforts in coalescence with the whole, that the whole product is a successful and well-utilized one.

People want to make things that they are proud of, and they want to be able to see this unfold–they want to be able to look forward, to focus on the outcome.

Being proud of yourself and the work you do is a large part of what makes a successful leader. It demonstrates that you not only are capable and confident in your skills but you inspire others around you. "Our research indicates that what really matters is that leaders are able to create enthusiasm, empower their people, instill confidence and be inspiring to the people around them," says Peter Handal, chief executive of New York City-based Dale Carnegie Training, a leadership-training company. Handal went on to describe **five keys for effective leadership.** They are to **face challenges, win trust, be authentic, earn respect, and stay curious.** We will discuss these topics in more depth later on but the general takeaway from Handal's message is that internal motivation shines through to become external motivation. This passion and confidence in your skills is transferred to your peers and coworkers through tangible and specific organizational outlets meant to increase overall efficiency and quality, such as through setting stretch goals, developing subordinates, engaging in highly collaborative behavior and encouraging innovation in those around them.

Good leaders are instinctual. They thrive on being able to maneuver in the moment, devising solutions to the problems around them from intuition based on past experiences. As an instinctual leader you should be working towards the big picture by moving fluidly through the moment focused on the outcome you envision. Being able to confidently and consistently empower those around you allows for progressive upward mobility. This requires you, as a leader, to be able to effectively maintain and communicate your vision for success to those around you, both internally and externally.

Stretch goals are an excellent form of external motivation, setting a standard for inspiration for your team which can be executed in a variety of fashions. You could create a compelling vision and then meet with team members to have them collectively set the goal, or encourage the team to find an ethical goal that focuses on the organization's mission.

Alternatively, you could call a meeting and deliver a classic half-time locker room speech, then allow them to set the goal. It is up to you how you want to bring to your peers and subordinates the energy and passion that you have within yourself, but it is vital in ensuring constant progress.

Sometimes, however, the constant push forward can be tiring, and maybe it seems like no matter how hard you work, there is no progress being made. You may start to feel as if your creative vision is fading or faltering, that you are not adapting quick enough to be relevant and as inspiring as you used to be. This can be disconcerting, and detract from your own personal journey for personal and professional success.

My advice is to not get caught up in trying to reach that mythical "next level." Everywhere you look there is another blog post, podcast or salesperson trying to convince you that they are all you need in order to take your leadership skills and your organization to the "next level," but it does not exist. There is only the next stepping stone towards your goals. As a pragmatic and effective leader you should understand and envision the success of your business and personal life, but you should also be able to express it in terms of goals. By defining a clear and easily communicable path to follow through specific, personal and progressive goals, you not only provide yourself with a pathway for success but one which others around you can model and learn from. Again, it comes down to putting your focus on the outcome you want in powerful and transferable ways.

Imagine that you are playing chess with a friend. You have been placed in a frustrating position, and there are no apparent good moves for you.

Do you:
• get angry and tip the board over?
• complain that you are not good at chess or anything else in your life?
• get up and leave the game?

Or do you study the situation, think about your options and make the best move?

You probably know somebody or multiple somebodies who are prone to the first three options, and I'm sure that their behavior has often been described as over reactive. After all it's only a game. To take it too seriously and overthink the problem can make it become stressful, which translates into paralysis (indecision). Every situation allows for a logical next move free from this paralysis, should you choose to let go of your ego, pride and emotion in regards to making your next decision. Focus on the next move while keeping your end goal in mind, and do not let deviations in progress affect your overall vision. By maintaining a clearheaded and results-oriented perspective you will be less likely to make decisions out of stress or apparent necessity. You'll be more capable of studying the situation, weighing your options, and making the best move based on your current pieces. You'll be able to adapt your vision without changing it entirely. You'll maintain focus on your outcome.

This is why minimizing decision-making the night before each work day is so incredibly important. The brain is like a muscle; when it gets depleted it gets less effective. When you focus on a specific task for an extended period of time, you are utilizing your executive function mental muscles, diminishing the limited capacity for extended executive function that you need in order to perform optimally at critical points.

By minimizing minor decisions and creating order and function in the world around you, your capacity for assisting others in a way which is both positive and efficient is maximized.

As a leader whose job is to motivate, inspire and innovate, all of your time is valuable, not just when you are on the clock. At the end of the day there are only so many things that you can expend meaningful energy on before your actions become less deliberate and more robotic. You slip into a routine, and the actions are no longer organic or catered to the needs of your objective and responsive to the minutiae which encompass the greater scheme of your success.

Remember, consistency derives quality over the long term through refinement. There is always a difference between somebody who has just started a job and one who has been at it for thirty years. So it is with painting, and so it is with leadership. But, as with any aesthetic endeavour, it is success with a variety of approaches that truly encapsulates what it means to progress. To be willing to experiment with the mold in such a way that it is improved, not broken, and to allow your subordinates that same freedom allows for you to let go of the less important day-to-day decisions, allowing you to focus on the larger goals ahead.

In order to keep yourself steady in the wake of life's unexpected happenstances, try to view life as a game. A game of strategy, the key being to successfully manage your resources. Successful players put their resources in the right areas, and pay attention to their health, energy and willpower. Being a potent motivator only works when you have the energy and stamina to approach life from an objective standpoint. When we are weakened by long days and extended mental fatigue, we are incapable of making an impact on the world around us as we should. We are replenished slightly by eating and fully by sleeping, but we are also constantly draining our willpower throughout the day. Every decision we make costs us a little bit of willpower, and ones where you must put aside something that you'd really much prefer to do instead of something you need to do require a lot of it. In order to slow that drain, you must ensure that you take care of yourself. If you are hungry, exhausted, or overworked, your willpower will falter and sputter to an ineffective halt. Spread your tasks out over multiple days, mix more demanding ones with less demanding ones, while prioritizing the most important tasks. Lastly, reduce your distractions so that you can focus on your priorities.

If you are reading this, you're likely already on your way to success. You've already got it in your head that there are things that you can change in order to further develop yourself and your skills. You're probably already aware that we have approximately 28,000 days to live, and every single one of them steers us onwards in whatever direction we've chosen. Focus on what is in your control, progress, and treat life like a game. Taking it too seriously gets us caught in that grouchy space where everything feels hard, wrong, or difficult. Seeing life as a game reorients our perspective, distances us from our ego and allows us to make objective decisions which ultimately are to our benefit.

When we absorb ourselves too personally in our work the successes and failures feel much more extreme. Being objective allows us to move onto the next goal more easily by allowing us to see mistakes as the momentary setbacks that they are. If we do make a wrong decision, we can simply make a new one. Peers, subordinates and superiors alike are influenced by a strong leader who is unafraid to pursue their vision (the outcome on which they are focused) despite setbacks, and further inspires those around them to develop their own skills further.

Chapter 7

Be Tolerant and Empathetic

In this chapter you will learn more about the importance of those around you and those that follow you. As a leader you must actively create relationships with those around you and strive to maintain these relationships, as they will aid you on your path to success. The first step to forming a good relationship is giving recognition to those around you for the work that they do and outlining the significant purpose that they serve to the group. You must covet these relationships by being a good listener when they have something to say, and giving respect to their opinions, their ideas, and their efforts. If you do this, you will form lasting bonds with your followers and those around you that will be crucial in your journey to becoming a successful leader.

Forming and maintaining relationships with your followers is a key aspect in your journey that will allow you to grow as a leader. You may think that it is good enough to simply inspire people through your acts of leadership and continue to gain followers in this manner. While this is definitely a good thing, the mark of a true leader lies in your ability to communicate individually with your followers to let them know that they are more than just a face in the crowd. If those around you feel appreciated they will put all of their effort into helping you reach your goals.

The main point that you must consider in the acquisition of loyal followers is that they all desire recognition. Every person on this earth, on some level and in some way, simply wishes to be accepted. As a leader you are a figure that those around you look up to, and you have the power to make them feel accepted and appreciated. In order to obtain a group of valuable and loyal followers you must provide them with individual recognition for their work. This will show that you care about them and that they matter in the grand scheme of things.

A good way to begin showing recognition to your followers is by introducing yourself individually and learning their names. Making a point of introducing yourself to those around you will show them that you are more than just a leadership figure to be idolized; it will show them that you are human just like everyone else. This simple action of introducing yourself will mean a lot to your followers as they will feel lifted up to your level.

For example, imagine yourself coming into contact with your favourite celebrity. If they approached you and produced a genuine introduction, and showed that they cared about you as an individual, it would make your day. It would be a memorable experience, and you would carry a positive opinion of that celebrity for the rest of your life. An introduction may seem like a simple and pointless action to you but it means a lot coming from a leader.

If you introduce yourself and learn the names of your followers, they will feel greatly appreciated and they will believe that they know you on a personal level. This is important because it will show others that you have great interest in your followers. If they understand that you are interested in them as individuals and not just as followers, they will prove to be even more useful to have as allies to your cause.

However, learning the names of the people around you is only the first and most basic step in the effort to show recognition to your followers. To make them feel truly appreciated, you must recognize not just their existence, but their efforts as well. There are a few steps that you can take to ensure that you are providing adequate recognition for the work that others do for you.

First, as a leader, you must recognize when someone performs an exemplary task and highlight that person's achievement. It is essential to provide recognition in a moment when someone is performing exemplary work, or directly afterwards. If you provide recognition long after someone's work has been completed, it will seem like you are congratulating them as an afterthought and it will not have nearly as much impact as it would if you had approached them in a timely manner.

Furthermore, for this form of recognition to be effective you must make sure to only reward those that deserve it. Your recognition will become less and less meaningful to your followers if you start congratulating people on doing simply that which they have been tasked to do. You must only make a point of recognizing those who put in effort above and beyond that which is required. Thus, your followers will put in more effort and provide better work in the hopes of gaining your approval and your recognition.

As a leader you must also take into account the context of the work that others are doing when you choose to give them recognition. Telling someone that they are doing a good job is not a bad thing by any means but it will mean a lot more to someone if you relate their success to the goal that you are trying to achieve. It will mean a lot to someone if you show them that you notice they are doing a particularly good job at something, but it will mean more to them if you explain why their role and their effort are essential to the greater cause. If you provide others with recognition and show them that they are an essential member in the journey to achieving your vision, they will feel a sense of fulfillment they will continue to provide quality work.

The next key aspect in providing meaningful recognition for your followers is to be authentic. As a leader you must be sincere in your praise as it will mean a lot to someone if they know you are truly impressed with their work. Branching off of this, it is important to learn which achievements deserve recognition, and how much praise you should give for certain actions. Your recognition and your praise should always be appropriate to the situation; it should match the effort and the results. If you continuously provide praise that is over the top in comparison to the effort that others put in, your praise will become meaningless. This is why you must keep a strict regime; only give praise and recognition to those that deserve it, and always give the correct amount based on the task that has been completed or the effort that has been put in.

One glaring error that many leaders make is to reward work effort with a certain monetary value, such as a gift card or a dinner voucher. As a leader you must avoid attributing the efforts of your followers to a monetary or material value, as this will show them that you can assign a number value to their usefulness and they will inadvertently feel limited.

Praise and recognition that comes directly from you, someone that they look up to, will mean a lot more to your followers than the demeaning nature of a material reward. In essence, your followers will join your cause because they believe in you as a leader. You are a role model for them because they know that you are strong, you stand up for your beliefs, and you have the ability to create positive change in the world. This is why praise that comes directly from you is priceless in their eyes; the goal of your followers is to help you to achieve your vision and to make you proud, and if you show that they have done this, they will feel a sense of meaning and accomplishment.

Giving recognition to your followers is a necessary first step that you must take as a leader in order to form meaningful and lasting relationships with them. If you covet and preserve these relationships, and continue to develop them, you will possess a loyal group of followers that use you as a source of inspiration and view you as a strong and successful leader. Thus, you must take the necessary steps to further the relationships that you have started by providing recognition to your followers for their various efforts.

As a leader the next step in furthering the relationships that you have with your followers is to show that you are there for them. Even though you are their leader you can show that you are personable, and willing to interact with those around you in a meaningful way. To do this you must learn the skill of being a good listener to your followers when they need your opinion, or simply when they need someone to talk to.

It may seem like a simple task, but there are many things that you must consider when you are attempting to be a good listener to one of your followers. Firstly, you must be sure to rid yourself of all distractions. For example, if you are trying to have a conversation with someone, and they keep pulling out their cell phone to check for messages from other people, it can be annoying and it can feel very disrespectful. You must enter a conversation with someone without any distraction, and make it known that your full attention belongs to them for the time being.

If you can truly focus on the person in front of you it will be clear to them that you care about them on an individual level. Thus, they will feel appreciated, and they will gain satisfaction and fulfillment from speaking to you. Another way to show that you are giving someone your full attention is to be sure to maintain good eye contact. Holding eye contact while listening to someone shows that you are earnestly taking in what they have to say, and that you are not devaluing their words by searching for distractions in different places around you. Eye contact is an intimate bond that shows others that you are a sincere listener.

As well as maintaining eye contact during a conversation, it is important to consider other types of body language in an effort to show that you are an attentive listener. You must not fidget or cross your arms as these are negative signs that can be interpreted as disinterest. Be sure to stay relaxed and calm, and devote your entire body towards the conversation at hand. If you master the skill of ridding yourself of all distraction and devoting yourself to a conversation, people will greatly appreciate you for it, and they will feel valued.

When entering a conversation with someone you must be sure to go into it with an open mind that is free of your own issues. If you wish to be a good listener you must simply be there with the intention to listen and take in what the other person is saying, not to pass judgment or berate them for their opinions. Try and empathize with those that you speak with because it is easier to understand someone's opinions when you can put yourself in their shoes. This will also help to show them that you value what they say because they will realize the effort that you are putting in to the conversation to understand their viewpoint.

To be a good listener you must train yourself to be an active listener. This means that you should not only be there for someone to listen to what they have to say without distraction; you should also be contributing to the conversation when it is necessary in order to fully understand and enhance their points. To do this you must learn to maintain a good balance between listening and contributing. Remember, when you are making an effort to listen to someone, the conversation is not about you; when you speak, it is only to attempt to further understand what they are trying to convey to you.

Being an active listener means asking appropriate questions. Do not interrupt the person that is speaking to you but if you do not understand something wait for the appropriate moment to clarify the point with them. Asking questions not only serves to increase your understanding of what they are talking about but it also helps the conversation flow and shows that you are interested, and that you desire to understand them.

Being an active listener also means that you must be emotive and expressive while someone is talking to you. If you respond in a neutral tone it may suggest to the other person that you are disinterested or bored. This is why you must engage in the conversation and show that the conversation is affecting you because you are really taking it in and truly listening. Do not be overly animated as this will come off as demeaning; rather, if you are successfully empathetic towards the speaker, you will find the necessary emotions will come easily to you.

Another major element that you must consider if you wish to become a good listener is the ability to remain open, and not to be defensive. As a leader you will have to have all kinds of conversations, some of them will be cheerful while others may be complaints or criticisms. You must not take it personally if someone that speaks to you gives you criticism or complains about your behaviour. As a leader you know that your decisions are precise and calculated but if someone has a complaint you still must give them your full attention without any reservations.

You will certainly have to deal with some difficult speakers in your time as a leader but if they know that you are a sincerely good listener, it will take some edge off of the conversation, and you will find a quicker route to an agreement or another positive outcome. If someone comes to you with criticism, you must convey to them that you are actively considering what they say to you, and that you are evaluating their actions. In this way, you will show them that their opinion matters and you do not dismiss your followers if they disagree with you.

As you can see, being a good listener has many advantages as a leader, and it is an essential skill that you must develop over time. The more experiences you have that call for you to be a good listener, the better you will get at listening to people and showing that you truly care about what they have to say. Being a good, active listener can show people that their opinions are important; it can make it easier for you to help them out if they are seeking advice, and it can even aid you in receiving criticism in a tough situation. No matter what kind of conversation you have, being a good listener will prove to those around you that you are a good leader because you care about your followers on an individual level, and you can find time to listen to what they have to say.

The last element that will likely seal the deal in the development of good relationships with your followers will be your ability to give respect to others. You are a leader, and these people follow you because they know that you fight for a worthy cause and that you have the ability to help large numbers of people. However, this does not mean that you are above them; it simply means that you are their guide. A successful leader is humble; you must know that all are equal even though many look up to you. Thus, you must respect your followers with the utmost integrity because they are the future leaders, and they are one of your biggest assets.

Giving respect to others is a broad notion, and it encompasses things like learning the names of your followers and being a good listener to them when they need you. Being respectful is a way of life, and it is an essential characteristic that all successful leaders must possess. If you are not respectful of others it will cause doubt among your followers that you are a great leader. All people are deserving of respect, and you as a leader should be the first one to give it to them.

One of the easiest ways to show respect to others is by conveying your gratitude for the things they do. You can do this by thanking people on a regular basis for what they have done for you, and the work that they continuously provide. It is a simple gesture that goes a long way in terms of how others feel towards you and it will make those around you feel respected and acknowledged. When people have this mindset they will continue to produce quality work, which is why your followers are one of your biggest assets as a leader.

A large element of your ability to give respect to others will be your idea of yourself as a leader. You must not think of yourself as being better than others simple because you lead them. Everyone in the world is equally deserving of respect, no matter their position. As a leader you must lead by example, and do the things which you expect from your followers and those that work for you.

For example, if you plan to have a meeting with some employees at work you must stick to the time that you set for the meeting. You may have other responsibilities to attend to but these other responsibilities will all be part of the planning process when you initially propose this meeting. If you set a meeting with your employees for, say, Friday at lunchtime, you must be there for the meeting at the correct time because this shows that you value the time of your employees just as much as you expect them to value your time and the time of those around them.

In this example, if you were to brush off the meeting last minute and reschedule with your employees, they would feel as if you value your own time far more than you value theirs. This is an act of disrespect, and it is not acceptable if you wish to keep your employees happy. You must lead by example; if you expect your employees to be on time for a meeting, then you should also have no excuse for being on time for that meeting. This will show your employees that you respect them and that you are on the same level as them.

To show respect to others you must be fair in your decisions. Just like you must not hold a higher opinion of yourself than those around you, you must also avoid holding certain colleagues in higher esteem than others. If you show favoritism among your followers, it will show them that there is a divide, and that you do not respect them all equally.

Giving respect to all of your followers equally is a key aspect in becoming a successful leader because all of your followers wish to receive that respect from you, and they will achieve fulfillment and be grateful to you if they do.

Showing respect to those around you also means going out of your way to help others. This is a duty that you have as a leader, and it will not only help you gain followers but help to preserve the ones that you already have. If you put all of your efforts into helping others they will be eternally grateful for it, and they will know that you respect them.

Giving respect to those around you is necessity if you wish to become a successful leader with a loyal band of followers. As you have learned, the benefits of giving respect are endless, and as a leader you will reap the rewards for these mostly simple acts that you can do for others. If you show respect to your followers they will produce better work, and they will bring you ever closer to reaching the goals that you desire.

To better understand the importance of respect, we turn to the great leader Martin Luther King Jr. Best known for his role in the advancement of civil rights through nonviolent means, Martin Luther King Jr. was one, of the greatest leaders in history based on his practices and his achievements. He was a leader in the African-American civil rights movement, and he achieved many great things throughout his career for the good of the people.

From a young age King was exposed to the awful realities of racism and racial segregation against black people in the United States. He lost out on many relationships due to the colour of his skin, and initially held resentment towards white people due to the racial humiliation that was felt by him, his family, and other members of his community. These early experiences are surely what sparked his later efforts to lead the African-American civil rights movement.

The event at which King delivered his most famous speech, "I Have a Dream," was the March on Washington in 1963. On August 28, 1963, hundreds of thousands of Americans stood in front of the Lincoln Memorial in Washington to hear Martin Luther King Jr. speak out on many of the issues that black people faced at the time. In his speech King called for an end to racism, as well as other more specific things such as an end to racial segregation in schools, meaningful civil rights legislation, and so on. This march is credited with helping to pass the Civil Rights Act of 1964, a great step in the right direction for humankind.

The main reason for citing King's great works is to outline the way in which he achieved his goals. The focus of his movement was on creating meaningful change through nonviolent protest, which showed a great amount of respect in a time where it would have been hard to muster. In the face of all of the injustices of the time King still managed to unite the people in a respectful protest, and this showed an incredible amount of restraint and leadership ability.

King would never have gotten as much exposure if his methods had been lacking in respect for society and the authority of the time. In essence, respect was the key factor in getting his message across to the world and achieving his vision. He created incredible positive change in the United States and in the world through the necessary characteristic of respect in his leadership.

In this chapter you have learned how to give recognition, be a good and active listener, and above all, how to give respect to your followers and those around you. This is an essential skill in your journey to becoming a successful leader as it will form lasting relationships and breed loyal followers. Furthermore, Martin Luther King Jr. shows us that having respect and being tolerant of others is a tough but necessary skill, and having the ability to hold these values will allow you to be a leader that is loved by many, and you will go down in history.

Chapter 8

Have High Energy

All of the stories and anecdotes that you have heard throughout this book have had a common theme which you will have noticed as you read through the lessons within these pages. This theme has been one of optimism and positivity, even in the face of impossible odds and numerous challenges. From the beginning of this book when we talked about discovering your purpose and thinking big to focusing on the next move while maintaining tolerance and empathy, we have maintained a high energy and a positive attitude all the time.

Of the many lessons which you will take from this book and add to your life, the overall lesson must be to maintain this positive attitude in all that you do. There will of course be times when you feel down, when life has trampled on you and when it seems like your plans have begun to fall apart. What sets apart those leaders who are seen as inspirational in times like these is the attitude that is maintained. When times are rough there will be those who just let things happen to them and there are those who lift their heads up and stride ahead with a determined smile on their face. It is those who can feel the pains of life and keep smiling, no matter what has befallen them throughout the day, who will succeed in the end.

Imagine for a moment that you are walking home from a long day of work, having started very early and given everything you have to the task at hand. You might feel exhausted, your legs ache, your mind is in multiple directions and all you want to do is fall into bed. And then, as you walk, a co-worker who did the exact same things as you since the morning comes by smiling and chatting. Somehow, this person has managed to keep a positive attitude no matter how out of energy they may be. And what do you feel? You feel inspired! You feel like this is someone who has made the most of every minute of every hour of their day and they are still giving everything they have. Soon after, you feel yourself smiling, too, with the laughter coming easily. These are the type of people that we look up to.

Now that person may not have felt like they wanted to smile, they may have very well wanted to do exactly what you did as well – to fall onto the bed and sleep deeply. But they gave that little extra effort that kept a smile on their face until the end of the day and in the minds of those that they met, that positive outlook will have raised them to a level above the rest. It's people like this that we see as leaders because they can go through all the daily struggles of life and still inspire a change in the rest of us when we are at our lowest.

This positivity is the mindset which you must adapt if you wish to be seen as a leader to those around you in your journey through life. I know that it may be tough, I know this well, there are days where I don't want to smile. I'll have had a bad morning, a tough afternoon and a horrible day overall. But throughout it all I make sure that I keep optimistic and bring up those around me because I know that I can make an impact to those I encounter if I do so. By creating this positive aura around yourself you will find, in time, that it is entirely possible to guide those around you to help build the world you want because they will know you as a positive guide in their lives. Even if all you start with is a smile each time you encounter someone else, it will soon grow over time—you will find yourself caught up in the positivity you have created in others which in turn will grow to make you smile more.

As you become more and more used to this daily habit of creating optimism in those around it will grow into something else, something stronger. It will grow into courage. Because of this you will find that control of your everyday life comes more easily. With courage comes determination, with determination comes discipline, and with discipline comes success.

As Aristotle, the famous philosopher said, "We are what we repeatedly do. Excellence, then, is not an act, but a habit." This can be seen in so many different self-help books but you need not read hundreds of pages to know this simple fact; it is in our daily habits that we can make the longer term changes in our lives.

It is through daily additions that we create a better life for ourselves, in a principle that I call the 1% principle. It is very simple. Every day you will aim to be better than you were yesterday by just 1%. One percent better is such a small difference that you will barely notice it.

Consider, for example, that you want to one day become a great writer. You start by writing just 100 words that first day. The next day you write 101 words; then the next day, 102. Over time all you have to do is reach where you were the day before and then a little bit more. By holding yourself to this principle, over time you increase bit by bit and soon enough your "1% daily increase" will have grown. Consider, by the time you reach 200 words a day, that 1% increase is going to be two additional words instead of the one you began with. You will look back weeks from now and realize that your 1% increase each time you write will result in what used to be 5% or 10% of your daily output. Then, you will realize how far you've come.

The numbers will change between each and every person and in each and every case things will change. A writer, a painter, a doctor, a journalist, a builder, it doesn't matter what you are trying to become you will become 1% better each and every day. By committing yourself to this increase you continually raise the bar on what you see as your standard. Trust me when I say that this is the best possible way to improve yourself not only as a leader, but as a human being.

I challenge you now to try something. Pick one habit that you have wanted to add to your life and write it down. Now, get a piece of paper and divide it into 28 squares—a seven by four grid. Today will be day one. Say for example that the habit you have wanted to start is daily exercise—it does not matter what you do as long as you do some sort of exercise that day. When you do, cross off the first box in your grid with one big "X". The next day, you will exercise again, maybe not a massive run or gym session, but some stretching to get the muscles ready before a long day of work. That is day two, so go ahead and add an X to the next box, right after the first day. Now you have two. The next day you keep it up because now you have the beginnings of a chain. You don't want to stop now because this is the beginning of something new, something that will last. And so over time you begin to form a daily habit that lasts and starts to become part of you. This builds into the 1% that I was talking about, that slow daily increase, as you build yourself into something stronger. And soon enough you have already reached a full week of the habit. You don't want to mess it up now! And so it becomes easier the next week and then the next and the next until suddenly – you've made it a whole month!

Many cultures have many different ways of sharing the same piece of wisdom; the first step is the hardest. It's so true because it's far easier to sit and dream all day of how much better that your life could be rather than focusing on how much better you can make it be. Daydreams and wishes are the foundation on which you will become a leader which others can follow, but this is only the beginning. Solid action is the true building blocks which can create a better life for yourself and your family. Without moving thoughts into decisions and decisions into change, it is impossible to become the leaders that we are all capable of becoming. So many people miss out on this crucial lesson and never manage to realize their dreams because that's all they had– hopes and dreams rather than plans of action.

Now, we have already spoken about the first two qualities which are necessary for a leader to hold in order to fulfill their true potential: **optimism** and **persistence**. The third characteristic which we shall seek as leaders is **courage**.

Courage combines not only the upbeat and forward looking bonuses of optimism, but it also includes the gritty determination of persistence. These two forces combine in the value of courage which is something that heroes and leaders from so many stories, both fictional and real, have held. Martin Luther King Jr. held immense courage in order to make the change in America for civil rights. Gandhi was courageous in the face of many obstacles throughout his mission for human rights. Nelson Mandela showed courage in his actions before prison and especially in his decades of confinement when he still made an impact on the future freedom of black people within South Africa.

What is also necessary to understand is that one must have all three of these attributes together to truly become a competent and inspiring leader. Only when all three are combined will you be a beacon of guidance to those around you. Consider for a moment what happens when you lack one of these components.

An optimistic person with courage will have a great start, much like the Hare from Aesop's Fables earlier in the book, which started the race far quicker than the Tortoise. However, lacking any sort of persistence, he fell behind and lost in the end. Someone who lacks persistence is like a firework—they might start with a bang and a lot of flashy lights but soon they will die out and fail.

Second, courageous and persistent people are an interesting mix because they are determined and will strive for what they want, but without optimism they can often become self-interested and inwardly driven. Without an outward sense of optimism people like this have a tendency to become materialistic and, while rich, they are not inspiring individuals to be around. For anyone who is hoping to be a leader to those around them it is clear that optimism is necessary as well.

Third, one who is optimistic and persistent but lacks the courage to fully strive for their ambitions might be a very good worker and will help others through the day, but they will fail to reach their true potential.

Without courage no one can become great because it is a key ingredient that causes us to truly pursue our dreams and make a change in this world. Courage drives us forward, makes us aim higher, dream bigger and makes us want to leave an impact on this world. Courage is the force which says deep inside you "I want to leave this world better than when I found it."

With all three of these attributes in place you can truly become a leader to those around you. This combination of qualities will take you far in life—be it in your career, your relationships or even simply in your day to day challenges. In the end you must always focus on keeping your head up, your heart strong and your persistence unwavering. As Gandhi said, "Be the change you wish to see in the world."

Chapter 9

Be Charismatic and Influential

In this chapter you will learn the vital importance of creating a positive atmosphere and a fun-filled environment for yourself and those you work with. It is important to keep a healthy balance of work and fun with those around you because this keeps people motivated, passionate, and productive. Once this space of positivity is achieved you must then learn to embody the change you want to see in the world, and others will follow you in your vision. To do this you must learn the values of sincerity and integrity so that people will see you as someone to look up to. Once you learn these skills you will be a more influential leader, and you will pave the way to success.

As a leader it is important to keep in mind the happiness of those around you, and especially those you work with. This is because happy workers will work better, which will bring you closer to the vision that you are trying to achieve. As you learned earlier on in this book, having passion for your own work is a key aspect in producing good results and achieving your goals. This is why you must breed passion amongst the people you work with if you wish to be a successful leader. The first step you must take in order to create a positive atmosphere for yourself and those around you is to make sure that you as an individual are happy and positive. You must show that you are passionate for the work that you do, and that you do not think of it as a chore. Think of the goals that you are trying to reach, and think of your growing success as a leader, and you will feel fulfilled and happy.

If you do not find and covet individual happiness it makes it much more difficult for those around you to remain happy and positive. As a leader you are the one who sets the example for their behaviour, and you are a role model to them. If you are happy, and they can see that you are happy, then they will follow in suit.

In essence, the most important thing to consider when you are trying to create a positive atmosphere is your own attitude. If you are happy you will radiate a good attitude which will make others happy as well.

On the other hand, if you are unhappy and you do not possess a positive attitude, or even worse, if you possess a negative attitude, then the people around you will notice. It is your job as a leader to set the tone for the workplace so that everyone can work to the best of their abilities in the hopes of achieving your vision and the goals you set out to reach.

To give an example, imagine you are a student at school. If you walk into class with the other students, and the teacher is clearly in a bad mood, you will automatically be put at a disadvantage. If the teacher is in a bad mood, the class of students and the teacher will be put in conflict with each other, and this will create a bad learning environment.

As a leader you are the teacher in this scenario, and you should radiate positivity on a daily basis. If you imagine yourself as the teacher in this scenario but you possess a positive attitude, you will realize that it creates a great learning environment for the students because they know that you are there to help them. If you are the teacher, then your followers are the students, and you must preserve a positive, fun-filled, and happy environment for them so that they can show their true potential in the workplace.

In order to remain positive there are a few steps that you can take outside of simply showing passion and enjoying the work that you do.

The first step you must take is to put in place a clear barrier between your work and your personal life. For example, if you are having any problems in your personal life such as troubles with your significant other, or anything like that, you must not let it carry over to your work.

Think of the front door to your home as a kind of cleansing perimeter around your personal troubles. Once you leave the front door of your house to get to work every morning, you must leave your individual problems behind you and focus on your role as a leader and a role model.

If you carry your problems with you to your workplace your negative attitude will be contagious, and it will infect all those around you with a similarly negative outlook. It is important as a leader to preserve a firm barrier between these two aspects of your life in order to avoid a situation like this, as a negative atmosphere will reduce productivity.

Another step you can take in order to remain positive is self-preservation. This means getting enough rest every night, eating well and following a proper diet, exercising regularly, and keeping good standards of personal hygiene. If you are a healthy individual, you will feel good, and it will radiate a sense of positivity to others.

Furthermore, you must make sure that you present yourself in a professional manner. This does not mean that you have to wear formal outfits all the time but you must be sure to keep well-groomed in order to create an aura of positivity around yourself. If you look good you feel good and if you feel good it will make those around you feel good as well. Charisma is a necessary quality to possess as a leader, and it is something you must learn if you wish to succeed. Robert Brault, an American opera singer, says this about charisma: "Charisma is not just saying hello. It's dropping what you're doing to say hello". On your journey as a leader you have learned the importance of putting others before yourself and maintaining the happiness of those around you.

Charisma is a natural leadership quality that comes quite easily; you simply must show an active concern for the well-being of others while maintaining your place as a role model, and you will be seen as charismatic and worthy of the loyalty and admiration of those around you. Having charisma will make people aspire to be like you, and you will create happiness in the workplace simply by being there and making others feel empowered.

If you take these steps to becoming a more positive individual, you will notice a positive change in those around you as well. Maintaining a positive mindset for yourself will maintain a positive atmosphere in your workplace and for your followers. The next step that you must take after achieving this positive atmosphere is making the environment into a fun-filled environment.

To create a fun-filled environment in the workplace you must build and maintain relationships with those you work with, and encourage those around you to form these kinds of relationships with each other as well. Using team-building and trust exercises will strengthen the bonds between everyone in the workplace, and it will add a sense of fun to the work you do.

Furthermore, humor is a powerful tool that you must use to ensure the workplace is a fun-filled environment. Do not use it to divert attention away from the work at hand, as this will halt productivity and have a negative impact on the workplace. Rather, you must encourage everyone to laugh and have a good time while they work in order to ensure that everyone is having fun and no one is feeling bored, dispassionate, or disgruntled.

Once you have created a positive atmosphere and a fun-filled environment for yourself and those around you in the workplace, you can focus on whatever task is at hand. It is important to maintain this healthy and positive atmosphere because it will foster a team of happy.and motivated individuals who will work together to help you attain your goals. As a leader one of the most important things you can do is empower others, as you have learned earlier in this book, and maintaining a healthy workplace environment is a key aspect of that.

Now as a leader, you are a long way into your journey to becoming successful and attaining your goals. If you have learned from this book then you are now a strong and charismatic leader with a loyal group of followers who admire and idolize you. Your followers feel empowered by the premise that they can become future leaders, and they are united under one vision – your vision. They all want nothing more than to help you achieve your goals, as you have improved their lives and they look up to you as a role model.

Thus, you must embody the change that you wish to see in the world.

As a leader you have learned the importance of striving towards your vision and overcoming any obstacles in your way. You have learned that, as a leader, you can use your power to create change, whether it is individual change, changing the lives of people around you, or changing the world on a grand scale.

Whatever kind of changes you seek, you must now become that change. Rather than simply orchestrating change you must live and breathe your plan and your vision in order to attain your goals. This is all part of your growth as a leader; you must become the embodiment of positive change, and you will be more greatly admired and accrue even more loyal followers that are willing to give all of their effort towards your cause.

Becoming the embodiment of change is something that you will have learned over time through the culmination of all of these different lessons in leadership. It is important to remember the lessons that you have learned from the earlier chapters of this book because they are all essential in molding you into a successful leader, and being a successful leader means that you must first create positive change in yourself.

As an aspiring leader you should have been focusing on improving yourself initially so that you can present yourself as a role model to those around you. This is the only way people will follow you because they will see that you are strong and you have a clear vision, and you are willing to help them with their problems. If you change yourself into an entirely positive entity in all aspects of your life, then people will see you as a catalyst for positive change.

When you display the ability to create positive change in yourself, you will gain recognition for it from those around you. If you display positive individual change, you will be seen as a beacon of hope by your followers because they will know that you have the power to create change not only in your own life, but in the lives of all of those who look up to you. Thus, you will gain the ability to embody the change you wish to see in whatever endeavors you choose to pursue.

There are a few rules that you should keep in mind if you wish to maintain this state of perpetual change, as you should as a successful leader. The first rule is one that you have learned early-on in this book— you should constantly be examining your own behaviours and evaluating your own performance with constructive criticism. This will ensure that you are constantly changing yourself for the better. Being in control of your actions and constantly improving yourself is an essential skill that all leaders must possess, and it is one you must also possess if you wish to fully embody the spirit of positive change in the world. The first step to changing the world, as you know, is improving yourself; this will be your gateway to creating change on a large scale.

Changing yourself is such an important first step for creating change on a larger scale because self-improvement will fundamentally change how you view the world, and it will dictate how you feel and what actions you take in the name of your vision. If you are constantly re-evaluating yourself as a leader should, you will be constantly viewing your environment in new and unique ways that would never have been available to you in your previous state of mind.

If you skip this key step, and you attempt to create change on a large scale without first altering yourself, you will find that it proves to be very difficult. If you still possess many flaws that you have failed to address you will not be able to unite those around you as a leading example of what should be done. It is only when the people realize the positive changes that you have instilled in yourself that they will believe in your ability to create bigger changes.

Another rule that you must adhere to once you have established the practice of constant evaluation and critique of your leadership abilities is that you need to seize the opportunity and take action in order to achieve your goals. It is true that improving yourself is a requirement for creating change in other areas, but it is only half the battle. Once you have improved yourself, you must still remain in control and lead people with a purpose.

As you have learned you must always have a clear vision as a leader. With self-improvement as your experience and a group of loyal followers at your back you must take charge and act on this vision. Show those around you that you are not only capable of being a role model because of your self-improvement but you are also capable of spreading that experience to the masses and using it as a tool to achieve your goals.

People will follow you if they view you as a strong, successful leader that they can look up to. However, they will only remain loyal to you if you display a drive for change and proof of progress. You cannot lead successfully based on your self-improvement alone. You also cannot lead by making grand promises that seem to be perpetually out of reach. If you wish to continue your progression on the journey to becoming a successful leader, you must be decisive and actively lead your followers to create measurable positive change in the world. In essence, the only way you can become the embodiment of change is to display the individual qualities of leadership that you have learned over time, while simultaneously showing those around you that you can use those qualities to create progress towards your goals. The ability to use this culmination of all of your leadership skills is what will truly set you apart from the rest of the aspiring leaders, and turn you into an inspiration for the people. Your followers will believe in you, and they will want to do everything they can to help you succeed. This is why it is crucial to give them what they want and provide opportunity to progress and allow them to help you create change in the world. This will prove to be a fulfilling experience for both you and your followers, and it will show that you have grown into a successful leader.

It is vitally important that you learn and nurture the values of sincerity and integrity if you wish to become a successful leader with a loyal group of followers. These qualities will make you stand apart from the crowd even further because they reflect well on your character as an individual. You need to have these qualities to be a strong leader because if you display sincerity and integrity in the way you communicate with those around you, you will be greatly admired and it will also help to create the healthy environment which all leaders must strive towards. Sincerity is defined as "the quality of being free from pretense, deceit, or hypocrisy". It is clear that this is a good and necessary quality for a leader to have. If you are a sincere leader your followers and all those who come in contact with you will know that you are true to your cause and you do not make empty promises. The people will know that everything you say and everything you stand for is what you truly believe in. To be sincere, first and foremost, you must make sure you are clear in your communications and instructions to those around you. You must lay out your vision in simple terms and make sure that everyone understands what it is you need from them. Furthermore, you have to give others approval and make them feel appreciated—show your gratitude for the help they give you towards your cause and thank them in a genuine manner. These people look up to you as a leader, and sincere approval is what they crave when you ask for their help in any way.

When you assign duties to others in the workplace, make sure that you show that you have knowledge of others and that you care for them. Assign people tasks that you know they will be good at due to their strengths, and highlight these strengths when you communicate with them so that they know you are sincere. Do not be vague in your instructions or let people assign tasks among themselves because this shows disinterest. You must prove to those around you that you care about each and every one of them individually, and they will view you as a sincere and gracious leader.

The philosophy of sincerity ultimately does not allow you to fight for a cause that you do not believe in. Make sure that, as a leader, you are striving to reach goals that you know will benefit you and those around you. Do not fight for a cause if you cannot believe in it with all your heart because this will reflect poorly on you as a leader. If you use your instincts and your leadership experience to form your vision and your goals you will always be striving for something that you genuinely and sincerely believe in, and your followers will admire you for it and raise you up.

Integrity is defined as "the quality of being honest and having strong moral principles; moral uprightness", and also "the state of being whole and undivided." Integrity is closely tied with sincerity and it should be clear that this is another vitally essential quality that all successful leaders must possess. Without integrity you as a leader will not have the ability to truly lead because those around you will not be able to see your vision clearly.

In order to form a clear vision as a leader you must possess integrity in order to carry yourself as a strong and upstanding individual. You must be whole and undivided in your views so that you do not contradict yourself because this will confuse those around you and they will think that you are unsure of what you really want to do – a sign of weakness in a leader. If you possess integrity you will be able to fully and simply explain all of your views and decisions because you believe in them with all of your heart, and people will look up to you for being steadfast.

Having integrity means that you not only need to uphold strong and resolute views but these views also must be based on strong moral

89

principles. As a leader your views must be inherently good-natured in order for people to accept them. You are free to hold abstract views or beliefs that seem strange to people because you will be able to convince people to follow you over time by using your leadership qualities.

However, you will not be able to convince others to believe in you if your views go against their basic moral standpoints. As long as your views strive to preserve peace and positivity your followers will believe in you and consider you a strong and successful leader.

When someone has made a mistake, it is your duty as a leader to help them back on to the right path and explain what they did wrong. If you possess integrity you possess the ability to be completely honest with people. It is not a bad thing to tell someone that they made a mistake because, chances are, they will want to learn from you. As long as you communicate effectively and neutrally, showing concern and providing help, others will appreciate your honesty in pointing out how they could do something better, and they will thank you for it. Possessing both sincerity and integrity will better allow you to embody the change that you wish to see in the world.

In order to better illustrate the idea of a fun-filled workplace environment, and the idea of becoming the change you wish to see, we turn to Google, an American multinational technology company famous for their internet search engine of the same name. The company was founded by Larry Page and Sergey Brin in 1996, starting from virtually nothing when the two were still in university. Now, Google is a multibillion dollar company and is considered one of the most influential companies of the digital era.

Google's philosophy is "to create the happiest most productive workplace in the world", and they seem to be doing just that. With the use of bright and intuitive office designs work does not feel dull and boring like a lot of office jobs do. The offices are designed with rooms such as a meeting room that resembles a pub in Dublin, and ski gondolas in the Zurich office, just to name a couple. These designs are intended to maximize creativity and allow for the best possible work environment to increase productivity and create good quality work from the employees.

Furthermore, the work days at Google are scheduled to include fun activities on a regular basis, a lot of which is aimed at getting employees out of their office and interacting with each other. The opportunities the company provides allow for frequent breaks, facilities for wall climbing and other sports, and themed days such as pajama days and costume parties for Halloween. Each office is unique in its own way, and one location even has a slide to travel between floors in the building.

One office location boasts the use of a large complex constructed on a single floor to combat the mental barriers that are posed by having multiple floors in office buildings. Google as a company wants all of its employees to feel equal, and to feel like their opinions matter and they are encouraged to be creative and flourish. This kind of progressive thinking shows how Google strives to be the change it wants to see, and that the company is not afraid to be different.

As a leader if you successfully create a fun-filled and healthy work atmosphere, you and those around you will greatly benefit from it. The work you create will come easier and it will be of better quality. If you provide this for your followers they will look up to you even more and allow you, with their help, to embody the change you wish to see in the world.

Chapter 10

Act Fast, Act Bold

In this chapter you will begin by learning the importance of being in the moment. As a leader your actions in a stressful or chaotic situation are the true indication of whether or not you are strong and you possess the necessary skills. In any kind of crisis situation your decision-making must be precise and correct so that you can successfully lead others through a time of peril. After the initial crisis has been averted, it is your responsibility as a leader to stand up and take control of the situation, and to make it right and reassure all those who were involved that you have it under control. Then, as a culmination of all the skills you have learned throughout this book, you will have the ability to be the leader you need to be in any given situation.

As a leader you must understand that you will inevitably encounter huge issues that cannot be foreseen. I am not referring to the roadblocks that you learned about earlier on that you can calmly plan around and overcome. Rather, I am talking about the kinds of issues that cause panic and utter chaos. In these kinds of situations you must learn to act in the moment. You alone have the power to take charge of the situation, and it is your duty as a leader to do so.

Being able to act in the moment is a unique skill that can only be learned through experience with the help of your instincts, but it is a vital skill to possess as a leader so that you have the ability to dissolve a stressful situation. The people around you will look up to you for help in their time of need when they do not have the mental fortitude to think on their feet in a time of peril.

Let us consider the following example in order to better illustrate this concept. Imagine yourself working in an office with a small group of employees. One day, the microwave in the lunch room malfunctions while a man is trying to heat up his food, and it sparks and catches fire.

The man panics and runs out into the main office to frantically explain what has happened, and this creates an even bigger panic and a stressful situation.

You as a leader must take control when no one else can. The more time is spent panicking and yelling about the situation, the more time the fire has to spread through the lunch room. You know this, and while your employees are confused and scared you must take control of the situation and be in the moment. There is no time for you to panic like the rest of them you must keep a cool head, think on your feet, and decide what to do as quickly as possible.

In this situation, if you were to successfully take charge you would use an assertive tone of voice to make yourself heard instantly, and tell everyone to evacuate the office in an organized manner. You would delegate the most responsible employee to supervise this process, and to call the fire department immediately. Next, you would grab the fire extinguisher and enter the lunch room to assess the state of the fire.

If the fire has spread rapidly and the situation seems unsalvageable with only a fire extinguisher, you would evacuate the building like the rest of your employees and wait for the fire department to arrive.

If the fire is relatively small and contained to the microwave area, and it is safe for you to be in the room to use the fire extinguisher, you would put out the fire and unplug the machine when you were sure it was fully put out.

These are the kinds of spur-of-the-moment decisions that you will be required to make as a leader in a stressful situation.

The true test of leadership is how you would handle a situation such as this. You must make quick decisions while taking action, as there is.no time to plan and consider your decisions in a state of emergency.

There are a few steps you can take to make sure that you are handling a stressful situation to the best of your abilities.

The first step that you must take when you are presented with a stressful situation is to analyze what exactly is going on. You must ask yourself what the problem is, who is in trouble, and what tools you have at your disposal to combat the situation, and you have to do it quickly.

In the office fire example, a quick analysis of the situation would be that there is a fire in the lunch room of unknown severity, there are employees panicking in the main office, and there is a fire extinguisher in the closet. Taking in the situation like this will give you all of the information you need to make your next move.

Next, you must prioritize in order to decide what needs to be done in hopes of quelling the situation. In the case of the office fire, you and the other employees are the main priority, which is why the first thing you need to do is organize an evacuation from the building. These priorities will be different depending on the exact event that you are dealing with at any given time.

The second priority in that situation would be putting out the fire in order to save the office and the materials in it from being damaged. In the example given, the fire had not spread so it was a good decision to use the fire extinguisher to put the fire out. However, if the fire was larger and had posed a significant risk, there is no need to be a hero – simply wait for the fire department to arrive and forsake the office and its materials because the preservation of human life is the main priority.

Sometimes, others will be of great help in times of crisis but most times you should rely only on yourself and your leadership capabilities to overcome a tough situation. To recap, you must first analyze the situation you are presented with, then you must prioritize what it is you need to do in order to overcome it, and then take necessary action. This entire process should be completed as quickly as possible in order to diffuse the emergency situation. This is why it is called being in the moment because you do not have long to decide what to do in any such situation.

Remember that it is your bravery and your prowess as a leader that will help those around you get through these times of crisis. It is your responsibility to do your best in any given situation and help others through it. This kind of responsibility can be daunting, but as a leader you have the necessary skills to take it on. When you shepherd people through any stressful situations they will be eternally grateful and they will call you a true leader.

After a crisis situation has been averted due to your intervention, it is your duty as a leader to stand up with responsibility and assess the aftermath of the crisis. You must put the well-being of others before yourself and make sure that everyone involved is okay. If anyone is injured then it is your job to arrange help for them, such as a trip to the hospital if necessary.

Overall, your main concern at this point must be to reassure everyone involved in the stressful situation that the worst of it is over. Let them know that you are there for them to provide any assistance within your power, and they will admire you for it. Selfless acts after chaotic events such as this are what separate the leaders from the followers. You must show those around you that you are a true leader by being there for them before you worry about yourself.

Going back to the office fire scenario, it would now be your job to find the rest of the employees wherever they went after evacuating the building, and make sure everyone is alright. You would address them in the same authoritative yet calm voice that you used during the event, and let them know that the fire has been put out. The responsible thing to do in this scenario would be to wait for the fire department to arrive and properly inspect the office for further hazards, just to be safe. As a leader you would wait with your employees outside until the fire department arrived, and then await further instructions from them.

While you are waiting, it would be your task as a leader to console those that were involved in this stressful event and to reassure them that everything is fine. You would address them as a group to let them know the status of the situation, and then you would approach them individually to make sure they are relaxed now that the initial chaos of the situation has subsided.

As a leader, when you are reassuring people in this way that have just undergone a highly stressful event you must be sure to come off as sincere and protective. Making eye contact and physical touching are both very reassuring, and it will mean a lot to someone who has just had to experience such a situation. Make sure you address all those involved individually, and see to their personal needs, should they have any. In the office fire scenario, no one is injured but people may be still recovering from the adrenalin and the stress of the event, and they will appreciate your support. You should pay close attention to the man who first reported the fire, as he is likely the person who is most deeply affected by this situation out of anyone in the group. As a leader you must make sure to tell him that he did not do anything wrong; it was merely an accident, and the office did not retain any significant damage from the fire. The bottom line is that he may feel responsible for this accident but you must combat his guilt by making him understand that it was out of his control.

Your charisma as a leader will be a great help to you in situations where you must console those who have undergone a stressful unforeseen event. Use of humor to diffuse the tense mood is a good way to guide everyone back to feeling normal and safe. You must focus on making those around you feel at ease, and laughing it off is a great way to make that happen.

As a leader you must also assume responsibility for making sure that any damage is fixed promptly after an unforeseen event has occurred.

Your first priority after the stressful situation has been diffused should be to console anyone who was involved, and fixing any damage should be a close second to that once you are sure that everyone is accounted for and provided with any help they need.

Thus in the office fire scenario, once the fire inspection has been completed and the building has been cleared your first job as a leader would be to look into repairing any damage that the lunch room sustained. This means you would likely have to oversee the counter being repaired, the wall being painted, and definitely the microwave being replaced.

This scenario of the office fire is a relatively simple event to handle as a leader but you never know what to expect in the realm of these kinds of scenarios. Do not let your guard down, and always be prepared to take charge should an unforeseen situation arise. Your followers will look to you to guide them through a tough time if they are too helpless to act on their own, and you must be there for them whenever they need you.

Perhaps the most definitive test out of everything that has tested your leadership thus far is the test of leadership in any given situation.

Essentially, to be seen as a truly great leader that is successful in all aspects of your life and your accomplishments, you must be able to provide the correct action for those around you based on whatever situation you find yourself in. You must be the leader that you need to be based on the requirements of the task before you.

This means that you must possess the ability to analyze a given situation, and provide the type of leadership that you perceive to be needed in that situation. This is based on many things including the scenario itself, the needs of your followers and everyone around you at the time, and your own personal beliefs. It is a culmination of all of the leadership skills you have learned thus far, and you must use these skills hand-in-hand to critically evaluate a situation and deliver a response that is needed, and one that will gain the approval of those around you.

The hopes of gaining the approval of others with all of your decisions should not mean you forsake your own beliefs to tell the people what they want to hear. As a leader you must know the correct action to take during any given scenario based on the n needs of everyone involved. If this means taking an action that others do not approve, so be it; you are a true leader and your skills will let you know the correct decision. If the people oppose it, you know that with time they will come around and be convinced of the benefits of your decision because you know it is the right one.

This takes us back to the life of successful leader Abraham Lincoln as he guided his people through the American Civil War. Lincoln had to make a tough decision at this time—to keep fighting for his cause, or to cut his losses and avoid casualties. It must have been incredibly difficult seeing all of the troops he had lost in battle but he knew that the correct decision was to press on and win the war because he believed in his cause, and he knew it was the best thing for his people.

I am sure that many opposed the way Lincoln fought this war, and many leaders have those who oppose them. However, the fact is that Lincoln's perseverance paid off, and the majority of people were grateful for it and admired him even more. He found a way to win the war and abolish slavery, even with a lot of opposition, but he succeeded in making a positive change that will resonate for millennia.

Lincoln had the resolve as a great leader to continue fighting for his beliefs in a time of war, and this is what separates him from other less impactful figures in history. He proved that he had the ability to be the leader that he needed to be at the time. Even if the country's opinion was divided, he knew that slavery must be abolished if we were to progress as humans on this planet, and he fought for it and got what he wanted; what the people deserved.

This is the kind of quality that you must possess if you wish to be seen as a truly great leader that will go down in history. You must be able to be the leader that you need to be based on the situation, and you must simultaneously become the leader that those around you are calling for.

This will increase your status as a leader by showing you have concern for the well-being of your followers, but you also make the right decision based on your own beliefs and values when a situation calls for it.

Maintain this balance, and you will be viewed as a successful and great leader for years to come, and your group of loyal followers will only continue to grow.

A good example of a leader who managed to be there for others and be the leader he needed to be in a time of need is Rudy Giuliani, the mayor of New York City during the 9/11 terrorist attacks against the World Trade Center towers. Giuliani reportedly played a visible role in he response to the terrorist attack, and received great praise for how he handled the situation. He was there for the people when they needed reassurance in that time of great crisis in 2001.

Mayor Giuliani was highly visible during the aftermath of the September 11, 2001 terrorist attacks. After the horrific events had occurred, Giuliani took control of the situation and coordinated the response of various city departments, as well as gaining support from other state and federal organizations. He then led these departments in carrying out anti-terrorist measures across New York, and began overseeing the restoration of the destroyed infrastructure of the World Trade Center towers and the surrounding area that was also affected.

Giuliani not only took it upon himself to organize relief and response for the destruction caused by the attacks but he also took responsibility for the welfare of the people of New York. He made frequent appearances on radio and television on the day of the attacks, and many times following that. He used this mass exposure wisely and kept the citizens of New York updated on the actions he was taking, such as closing tunnels as a precautionary measure.

Giuliani also used this airtime to reassure the people that the worst was over, for example, he stated that there was no reason to believe that the dispersion of chemical or biological weaponry in the air was a factor in the attack. Giuliani was essentially the voice of the people, and that is what they needed most at the time. It was a horrific event for the entire world, most of all the citizens of New York, and Giuliani did a stellar job at uniting his city to rebuild itself and remain strong in the wake of the unforeseen terrorist attack.

After the attacks, Giuliani was hailed by many as a great leader for his actions during and after the crisis. When polled just six weeks after the terrorist attacks, Giuliani received a 79% approval rating from the voters of New York City, a drastic increase from the 36% approval rating he had received a year prior to these events. This goes to show just how important these times of crisis can be for the development of leadership.

Giuliani was praised for the professional manner in which he handled this situation, seeing to the needs of his city and his people, because he was the leader that he needed to be.

In his many public statements, Giuliani's words resonated with the feelings of New Yorkers after the 9/11 attacks. He displayed the same reaction that they did – shock, sadness, anger, the necessity and the desire to rebuild the damage done to the city, and a longing for justice to be served to those that were responsible for the attacks. He spoke these powerful words on the subject: "Tomorrow New York is going to be here, and we're going to rebuild, and we're going to be stronger than we were before…I want the people of New York to be an example to the rest of the country, and the rest of the world, that terrorism can't stop us." His speeches truly display an understanding of the needs of the people, and he provided the reassurance that they needed after these horrific events.

Mayor Giuliani showed his true dedication to the people of New York and the restoration of the city by fighting for an extension in his mayoral term due to the state of emergency, and demonstrated that he was willing to take on responsibilities far beyond what was expected of him. He was given the term "America's Mayor", coined by Oprah Winfrey at the 9/11 memorial service, due to his dedication to leadership in the time when people needed him most. Giuliani showed that he was dedicated to leadership in all aspects of the concept.

On December 24, 2001, Giuliani was named by Time magazine as its "Person of the Year." Time magazine noted that, prior to the 9/11 attacks, Giuliani's public image had been quite negative, depicting him as a self-righteous and ambitious politician. After the events where he displayed incredible leadership skills, his public image was reformed to that of a man who was able to unite a city in the middle of the greatest crisis it had ever faced. Regardless of his character blemishes from years before Giuliani stepped up as a leader when the people most needed him, and he was rewarded for it by gaining the loyal admiration of the people of New York, and many people across the world.

Giuliani perfectly emulates everything that you should have taken from this chapter in terms of the qualities of a true leader. He was able, first of all, to be in the moment, and lead the people of New York through a crisis of unimaginable severity. No one was prepared for the terrorist attacks of 2001 but he led the city through those horrific events in a professional and authoritative manner, addressing all concerns and giving the people what they needed.

Furthermore, Giuliani was able to take responsibility during this crisis; not only for his own duties, but for many things that were not necessarily his tasks to worry about. He showed that he truly cared for his city, and he showed it at the time when it meant the most. This made him stand out as a truly great leader compared to other figures in similar positions.

Lastly, and most importantly, Mayor Giuliani demonstrated that he was able to be the leader that he needed to be in this time of crisis, and he was able to be the leader that the people desired. What lifts Giuliani above other aspiring leaders is his capacity to oversee positive change in many different areas in the aftermath of the terrorist attacks. He demonstrated clear responsibility in his organization of response teams, and he showed empathy and compassion in his reassuring messages to the people. He made it clear that their interests and concerns were also his, and that he would do anything in his power to make the situation right again.

This is where your journey to becoming a successful leader truly begins, now that you have learned all of the valuable lessons on leadership from this book. All of the individual lessons are vitally important, but as Giuliani demonstrates, the most important thing of all when it comes to leadership is having the ability to be the leader that the people want, and doing what you know is right in the face of hardship or crisis.

It is important to know and possess the qualities of a leader on an individual scale, but it is arguably more important to put these qualities into practice in a stressful situation where you must take into account your responsibilities, the needs of the people, and the resolution of the situation. Being able to affect others and gain admiration from those around you for your sheer prowess in the leadership field will be the prime indicator that you are a successful leader, and if you reach this point, you will surely go down in history.

Chapter 11

Keep Everyone Motivated

Let's begin with keeping you motivated. To be seen as a leader at work, you'll need the drive to consistently deliver superior results. This means you'll have to find ways to maintain the energy reserves to give your colleagues a boost when they've had a tough day. You'll also want the mental agility to be able to deal with senior leaders at a moment's notice—so that they know you're up for bigger challenges.

Here are some suggestions to help you do that:

1. **Arrive at Work in a Good Mood**
    It has been found that call centre representatives who start the day in a good mood deliver superior results and feel more positive after their calls. Co-workers who arrive in a bad mood suffer a dip in productivity of up to 10%. Why? We now know that a positive mood lifts your brain's dopamine levels, resulting in improved cognitive performance. So, it just makes good sense to build a mood-lifter into your commute to work, whether it's listening to music or a motivational audio book, watching an uplifting TED talk, catching a highlight from your favorite late night show or having a conversation with a good friend. Make the effort to do whatever you can to ensure you walk into the office uplifted and ready to take on the challenges of the day.

2. Manage Your Energy, Not Your Time

Energy management has helped top athletes with their performance. I suggest you keep a log of your energy peaks and valleys for at least a week, and from those insights, build a new routine. By paying close attention, you might learn that your peak energy times are between 10 am and 2 pm, leading you to schedule your meetings or conference calls during those hours and to make the decision to begin having later lunches so that you can make the best use of that high-energy time.

3. Increase or Expand Your Performance

Once you've found your performance high energy times, I suggest working, for example, on that high-level presentation you have tomorrow for an intense 90 minutes, then shake things up with a stretch break or walk. Working smart like this allows you to actually extend or expand your capacity—just like athletes do.

4. Be a Motivator

Once you have all that energy, sharing it with others will motivate your team, as well as boosting your own performance. How, exactly, do you do that? Simply making eye contact establishes an emotional connection with the person you're speaking with. So, if you want someone to know he or she has your undivided attention, just put away your cell phone, lean toward him or her, and make eye contact.

When it comes to leaders motivating employees, surveys have shown the three most important issues are: respect, a sense of accomplishment, and recognition. Money is important but it is not as critical as these other components. So, taking these three issues into consideration, here are some additional ways to keep your team motivated:

5. **Involve Your Colleagues**

   Many employees want to be involved in the ongoing development and progress of their company. Plus, they often have insightful ideas that can make a significant difference in the company. And when they are involved, they buy-in faster and resist less. This means you can implement change(s) more quickly and easily.

6. **Communicate**

   Employees want regular updates on the progress of the business and their personal performance. Use memos, email, telephone, in-person meetings to keep your team apprised. Let them know if the business is on track. Tell your colleagues and/or employees what challenges are currently being faced (they may have suggestions). It is also important that you give them feedback on their performance. If you have a concern with a specific component, tell them and give them the opportunity to correct their behavior. I am always surprised how many employees do not receive feedback of any kind pertaining to their performance.

7. **Celebrate Individual and Team Performance**

   Catch people doing something right and focus on recognizing excellent performance. On an individual basis, you can provide positive reinforcement, issue awards, use a corporate newsletter to highlight specific achievements. Send thank-you, birthday, and anniversary cards as well as congratulatory notes. Make personal phone calls, and send emails. Better yet, if you work in a large organization, have a senior executive send the email or make the call. To recognize team efforts, post performance charts on the wall or throw an impromptu get-together. Treat them to lunch or a pizza party, post team pictures on your Intranet and in their work environment or give them plaques, certificates, coffee mugs, etc.

Ultimately, the more of these approaches you incorporate into your motivation strategy, the more energized your team will become. Make it a point to recognize someone everyday.

8. Set Challenging Goals

My experience has taught me that people strive to achieve what is expected of them. If you set challenging goals (like increasing sales by 15% this year) your team will work hard to accomplish them, providing of course, they are realistically attainable. It is amazing what people can accomplish when they are given the opportunity to perform. Communicate these goals and keep your team informed on the company's progress.

9. Give Them the Tools to Succeed

No team will stay motivated if they do not have the necessary tools required to do their job. This includes: equipment, internal support, inventory, marketing materials, training, etc.

10. Manage Poor Performance

Your team expects you to manage individuals who do not perform to standard or contribute fully to the efforts of the team. However, many managers ignore poor performance because they are afraid of the potential conflict. Instead, they hope that the situation will resolve itself. It never does and this "blind" approach affects profitability, causes higher turnover, and contributes to low morale in the workplace. While poor performance and conflict are seldom enjoyable to deal with, you have a responsibility to your team and the company to manage it. Here is the B.E.S.T. method of dealing with these situations:

Begin with the situation. "John, you are consistently late and the other employees see this."
Express the result. "This behaviour causes friction between you and your colleagues."
State the desired change. "Going forward, I want you to be here by 8 am or before."
Tell them the consequence. "If this behaviour doesn't change, I'll be forced to take further action."

11. Lead by Example

If you want your team to treat each other with dignity, you need to set the tone. If you expect them to be motivated and enthusiastic it is critical that you behave in this manner. As an owner, manager or business leader, your team looks to you for direction and guidance. Make sure they get it—as nature abhors a vacuum!

Here are some examples of motivational tactics that apparently work better than monetary rewards ...

12. Be Generous with Praise

Everyone wants it and it's one of the easiest things to give. Plus, praise from the CEO goes a lot farther than you might think. Praise every improvement that you see your team members make. Once you're comfortable delivering praise one-on-one to an employee, try praising them in front of others.

13. Get Rid of the Managers

Removing the project lead or supervisor and empowering your staff to work together as a team rather then everyone reporting to one individual can do wonders. Allowing people to work together as a team, on an equal level with their co-workers, will often produce better projects faster. People will come in early, stay late, and devote more of their energy to solving problems.

14. Make Your Ideas Theirs

People hate being told what to do. Instead of telling people what you want done, ask them in a way that will make them feel like they came up with the idea. "I'd like you to do it this way" turns into "Do you think it's a good idea if we do it this way?"

15. Never Criticize or Correct

No one, and I mean no one, wants to hear that they did something wrong. If you're looking for a de-motivator, this is it. Try an indirect approach to get people to improve, learn from their mistakes and fix them. Ask, "Was that the best way to approach the problem? Why not? Have any ideas on what you could have done differently?" Then you're having a conversation and talking through solutions, not pointing a finger.

16. Set the Bar High

Highlight your top performers' strengths and let them know that because of their excellence, you want them to be an example for others. You'll set the bar high and they'll be motivated to live up to their reputation as a leader.

17. Give Recognition and Small Rewards

These two things come in many forms: Give a shout out to someone in a company meeting for what she has accomplished. Run contests or internal games and keep track of the results on a whiteboard that everyone can see. Tangible awards that don't break the bank can work too. Try things like dinner, trophies, spa services, and plaques.

18. Throw Company Parties

Doing things as a group can go a long way. Have a company picnic. Organize birthday parties. Hold a happy hour. Don't just wait until the holidays to do a company activity; organize events throughout the year to remind your staff that you're all in it together.

19. Share the Rewards—and the Pain

When your company does well, celebrate. This is the best time to let everyone know that you're thankful for their hard work. Go out of your way to show how far you will go when people help your company succeed. If there are disappointments, share those too. If you expect high performance, your team deserves to know where the company stands. Be honest and transparent.

The bottom line, in my opinion, is engaging your colleagues and employees. Let them get to know you as a leader and make that process a positive and rewarding one. You'll be the leader you want to be in no time at all.

Chapter 12

Have a Sense of Humor

A sense of humor is part of the art of leadership,
of getting along with people, of getting things done.
— Dwight D. Eisenhower

Your attitude is like a box of crayons that color your world.
Constantly color your picture gray, and your picture will always be
bleak. Try adding some bright colors to the picture by including
humor, and your picture begins to lighten up.
— Allen Klein

Tasteful humor is a key to success at work, but there's a good chance your co-workers aren't cracking jokes on a regular basis-and your office could probably stand to have a little more fun.

Humor, by its nature, tends to have an edge to it, so people typically tone it down at work. It's hard to do well and easy to do badly. Plus, we all have a tendency to take ourselves way too seriously.

The amount or type of humor you'll find in any given workplace depends almost entirely on the culture. In workplaces that encourage people to be themselves--that are less hierarchical and more innovative--people tend to be more open with their humor. Even people who aren't always comfortable sharing their humor tend to do so in more relaxed environments where the use of humor becomes second nature with everyone's style.

Then there are workplaces with employees who tone down their humor, often with the desire to be taken more seriously. Yet, this can backfire as people who take themselves overly seriously are often, ironically, taken less seriously by the people around them.

Overall, employees are much more comfortable using humor with colleagues than they are with their bosses. You face a higher risk factor when joking around with your boss because you just don't know how your lightheartedness may be taken. So, you generally find greater reticence to use humor with senior managers.

Other reasons workers might hold back: A fear of offending someone; a fear of not being funny-that their humorous attempts will crash and burn; or the unwillingness to "get the ball rolling."

Many leaders, especially introverts, don't know how to safely encourage the use of more humor at work and are unsure how to express it in their own leadership style. Many of my clients also simply cite a lack of time as a key dampening factor. The desire is there, but they simply don't know how to bring more humor into their busy work life.

Whatever the reason may be, if you or your colleagues tend to be dry and dull in the office, you'll want to work on injecting more humor into your work day.

Many surveys suggest that humor can be at least one of the keys to success. A Robert Half International survey, for instance, found that 91% of executives believe a sense of humor is important for career advancement; while 84% feel that people with a good sense of humor do a better job. Another study by Bell Leadership Institute found that the two most desirable traits in leaders were a strong work ethic and a good sense of humor.

At an organizational level, some organizations are tapping into what I'd call 'the humor advantage. Companies such as Zappos and Southwest Airlines have used humor and a positive fun culture to help brand their business, attract and retain employees and to attract customers.

Humor demonstrates maturity and the ability to see the forest through the trees. You don't have to be a stand-up comedian, but well-placed humor that is clever and apropos to a business situation always enhances an employee's career.

People will enjoy working with you. People want to work with people they like. Why wouldn't you? You spend huge chunks of your waking hours at work, so you don't want it to be a death march. Humor—deftly employed—is a great way to win friends and influence people. You need to be funny, but not snarky (that's not good for team building) and you can't offend anyone.

Humor is a potent stress reliever. In fact, it's a triple whammy. Humor offers a cognitive shift in how you view your stressors; an emotional response; and a physical response that relaxes you when you laugh.

It is humanizing. Humor allows both employees and managers to come together, realizing that we all seek common ground.

It puts others at ease. Humor is a way to break through the tension barrier. Research shows that humor is a fabulous tension breaker in the workplace. People who laugh in response to a conflict tend to shift from convergent thinking where they can see only one solution, to divergent thinking where multiple ideas are considered."

Eureka! Humor is a key ingredient in creative thinking. It helps people play with ideas, lower their internal critic, and see things in new ways. Humor and creativity are both about looking at your challenges in novel ways and about making new connections you've never thought about before. Humor establishes a fertile environment for innovation because people are more inspired when they are relaxed.

It helps build trust. You can build trust with the effective use of humor because humor often reveals the authentic person lurking under the professional mask. Numerous studies suggest that people who share a healthy, positive sense of humor tend be more likable and are viewed as being more trustworthy. Humor is also viewed as sign of intelligence. All of these characteristics, as well as the fact that humor is a fabulous icebreaker and can tear down walls, can help people build relationships in the workplace, and especially these days, relationships are critical to success.

It boosts morale. Humor boosts morale and retention while reducing turnover because employees look forward to coming to work. Employees like to work for and with others who have a sense of humor. We all prefer to have fun at work. It should not feel like an indentured servitude environment.

People who use humor tend to be more approachable. The more approachable you are, especially as a leader, the more honest and open people around you will be. And the more honest and open people tend to be, the more successful and innovative teams tend to be.

Humor can allow your company to stand out. It can help companies stand out and go beyond with their customer service, garnering them a huge loyal following. If you want to stand out from the pack, using humor with your service is an effective way to do that.

It can increase productivity. Humor creates an upbeat atmosphere that encourages interaction, brainstorming of new ideas, and a feeling that there are few risks in thinking outside the box. All that leads to greater productivity. It also stands to reason that if you're in a more jovial atmosphere, you'll have more passion for what you do. Your work ethic will increase, and your enthusiasm will likely be contagious. It's a win-win for you and your employer.

Some humorous business quotes

The problem with the rat race is that even if you win, you're still a rat.
— Lilly Tomlin

The only place success comes before work is in the dictionary.
— Vidal Sassoon

If it's stupid but works, it isn't stupid.
— Unknown

By working faithfully 8 hours a day you may eventually get to be boss and work 12 hours a day.
— Robert Frost

The best way to appreciate your job is to imagine yourself without one.
— Oscar Wilde

A company is known by the people it keeps.
— Unknown

Notes

Notes

Notes

Notes

Notes

Notes

Notes

Notes

Notes

Notes

Notes